A Man Named *Daniel*

Other Books by Joseph Cone

A Common Fate: Endangered Salmon and the People of the Pacific Northwest. New York: Henry Holt, 1995. Paperback: Oregon State University Press, 1996.

Fire Under the Sea: The Discovery of The Most Extraordinary Environment on Earth–Volcanic Hot Springs on the Ocean Floor. New York: William Morrow, 1991. Paperback 1992.

A Man Named *Daniel*
The Remarkable Life of
Daniel Cone

Joseph Cone

Text & Context
Corvallis, Oregon

Text & Context, Corvallis OR 97333

For Dolores,
Mary-Jo,
and Adam

Contents

Illustrations

Afterward

Credits

Cover, Scottish National Portrait Gallery; p. 3, photograph by Margaret Van Patten; p. 4, illustration from *The Bulletin of The Society for the Preservation of New England Antiquities*. Volume XXII; July, 1931; Number I., courtesy of Historic New England; p. 7, map illustration by author. Google Map; p. 12, map courtesy Electric Scotland, http://www.electricscotland.com/webclans/clanmap.htm; p. 15, photograph from thescaledknot.org; p. 23, map reproduction courtesy of the Norman B. Leventhal Map Center at the Boston Public Library; p. 29, retouched from photo by Katya Kallsen © Harvard University, Winthrop portrait by unidentified artist, Harvard (Fogg) Art Museum portrait collection (converted to monochrome); p. 33 and 34: Courtesy of the Massachusetts Historical Society; p. 37, from M. Duhamel du Monceau, *Art du charbonnier. Maniere de faire le charbon de bois*, Paris: Chez Desaint & Saillant, 1761; p. 40, Mason A. Green, *Springfield 1636-1886*. C. A. Nichols & Co., Publishers, 1888; Courtesy Springfield City Library; p. 43, photo illustration by author from public map displayed at Tantiusques mine site; p. 48, Saugus Iron Works National Historic Site; p. 66, Courtesy of the Massachusetts Historical Society; p. 69, from watercolor previously at the Manor House in Gardiner Island from a July 2007 exhibit by the East Hampton Historical Society on Gardiners Island. Photo by poster. Public Domain by Wiki Commons; p. 82, The Execution of Charles I, engraving by "C.R.V.N.," 1649, (English) National Portrait Gallery (RN15997) Public Domain; p. 86, from John Underhill, *News from America*, Underhill Society of America, 1902; p. 101, Connecticut Historical Society (Hartford, Conn.); p. 103, 104, 107, photographs by author; p. 109, map reconstruction (top) by Richard M. Bayles; map (bottom) by Google.

Preface

Why do people become interested in the story of their ancestors? Interest in family history in the previous couple of generations—parents and grandparents—is understandable. Knowing more about them, about their characters, their choices, may help us understand more about ourselves. But ancestors, the people of your family name or blood who lived and died before your memory or the stories told to you – this is different.

The usual suspected interest, that somehow by knowing the old history you will discover something about your past that makes you more *important* or gives you more status, is, I think, overrated. By the time most adults become sincerely interested in the deeper past, they have reached an age in which their own identity and sense of place in society are set well enough that knowing the social status of their ancestors is unlikely to have any great effect on them.

Each person will place an individual value on "blood," on the importance of being genetically related to a particular ancestor. There is no denying the mystique of blood, of nature. But the farther distant in time one is from a particular ancestor, and the more spouses and descendants whose genes mix with and "dilute" those of the ancestor, the harder it is to make a rational case for the influence of this ancestral make-up. The fire of living, in all those individuals since the historic time, transforms the raw material of nature.

The real interest in knowing about ancestors, I believe, is rather of two kinds. Partly (for the investigator especially), the pleasure is in the investigation, the uncovering of old love letters and last wills, court records and frayed maps, newspaper clippings and faded photographs that may have been lost for generations if they were ever shared at all. Partly (for the reader especially), the pleasure is in the satisfaction of curiosity, of a sense of discovery, and sometimes a heightened appreciation for the circumstances of life and the difficulties of living that people endured who came before you, and to whom, in a sense, you owe your life. (*Really, he came to America as a prisoner of war? I had* no *idea.*)

For myself, I confess to both kinds of pleasure. As a college student, I discovered in an obscure book in a great library that I was the last in a direct line which contained not just one or two previous individuals bearing my first and last name but *six* Joseph Cones dating back to the turn of the eighteenth century. This was news to me, but the most I could make of the redundancy at the time was the hunch that my forebears had a charmingly quaint lack of imagination. However, the passage of a few decades has made me susceptible to a more generous explanation (though not necessarily more true). Perhaps these ancestors had a distinct feeling for family and history —a sense of continuity and their place in it.

My own father certainly did. Becoming a history teacher after the Second World War, Joseph Mortimer Cone spent many hours in private study and several family vacations taking his wife and children to celebrated locations where his ancestors had been part of American history: Haddam, Connecticut, where Daniel had helped start a community in the 1660s; Fort Ticonderoga on Lake Champlain, where the first Joseph Cone had probably fought during the French and Indian War; the battlefield at Gettysburg, where (my father believed) Union cavalryman Owen Sutton Cone had served and survived. Walking across this battlefield as a teenager, I learned from my father's absorption in its epic story of courage and unimaginable suffering, something new. Somehow, my father was able to ignite the immediacy of other people's lives, to convey by the spark of some detail, that although the time was long ago, that they had been vividly, precariously *alive*.

I have another reason for telling this story of Daniel Cone. I have a son who carries the family name but who knows little of the family history. I would wish that some day he might turn to this account with curiosity and pleasure and even a kind of contentment over those of his name who have come before. Knowing the story of a family, if its individuals are seen to be men and women who made the best of life as they knew how, overcoming difficult circumstances, can perhaps put one's own story into perspective and offer insights into that shared human journey which is the making of a meaningful life.

As the reader may wish to know about my qualifications to undertake this story, the essentials are that for more than 30 years I have made my living mainly as a writer, usually as a journalist and for most of that time in the specialty of science writing. For those unfamiliar with this craft, the key requirement of the science writer is an ability to translate the specialized languages and processes of science into terms that the non-specialist can understand. The craft also requires both a keen attention to evidence and proof and an ability to describe the living people who sometimes take refuge behind walls of facts. It has been my privilege to write about talented scientists in several fields who conduct their research investigations at a public university. All of this writing has been scrutinized by the researchers, edited by my professional peers, and held to high standards of accuracy and accountability by the university. Although writing about science may seem far removed from writing a family history, the discipline of the former, the reader of this book may hope, may inform the latter.

I would not want to give the impression that "science writing," at least as I have practiced it, is formulaic and bloodless. Quite the opposite. The two books I have written are what the publishing trade calls "non-fiction novels" with scenes, action, dialogue, and all the other common trappings of the novel, most importantly character. It is character which drives my stories. That my characters are real people alive today and very particular about the accuracy of how they are presented only underscores the reality that writing a non-fiction novel is often as challenging as writing the fictional kind.

As with many others interested in genealogy, I have benefited enormously from all the work that has gone before mine, much of which is these days more accessible than ever before because of computer-based digital libraries and digital resources, notably on the World Wide Web. There are many active genealogical researchers sharing information on the Web and more information online than was ever so readily available before. But the researcher still needs to apply standards of judgment about source materials with the same care and thoughtfulness that has always been required in historical research. The hard work of finding new information and of determining its value still requires old-fashioned digging in primary sources, most of it decidedly not online. All the most interesting primary materials I found for this book were located in old books and original manuscripts dating back to the 1650s. This book includes a bibliography and extensive list of notes, so the reader, too, may know my sources and weigh my handling of them.

Among a few researchers and writers mining similar materials, I want to acknowledge Diane Rapaport, whose previous work was a real help to me. And the librarians at the public libraries in Haddam and East Haddam, Connecticut, also deserve my thanks for guiding me to historical items in their collections.

Beyond these sources I want to especially acknowledge my aunt, Dolores Cone Qually, whose indefatigable enthusiasm for this project and supply of useful suggestions and links to the past were invaluable.

Introduction

Daniel Cone appears to be the first of that surname in the American colonies, arriving in Boston two decades after its settlement, almost certainly in 1652. Because of his early arrival, the distinctive spelling of his surname, and the number of children he sired who survived to bear children of their own, many present-day Americans trace their ancestry to Daniel Cone. As such, he is of interest, and previous genealogical works have touched on his life. However, none previously has focused on primary source documents with the intent to extract and elaborate as clear and full an account of his life as possible. Unless and until more primary documents are discovered, Daniel's descendants will need to be content with a biography that is incomplete. And yet, given the circumstances of his life and times, it's remarkable that there are enough documents to construct a satisfactory sketch of the man in his world.

A Scot, Daniel was very probably a prisoner of war who was deported and became an involuntary servant, or slave, in Massachusetts at about age 27. Arriving in the English colonies, he likely shortened his Scottish surname from something that sounded like MacCone to simply Cone. Fortunately for him, he served one of the most notable men of his time, John Winthrop, Jr., the son of the founder and governor of the Massachusetts Bay Colony, and himself governor of Connecticut Colony for many years. Largely as a result of Daniel's connection to Winthrop, documents reveal some of his life during the 1650s. As the normal term of servitude was seven or eight years, by 1660 or 1661 he would have been free from that obligation, and the events of the following years indeed speak to a greater freedom of choice. In 1662 he married, and by 1665 he was a founder of a new community, Haddam, on the Connecticut River. Legal documents give some glimpses of his life in his adult years of the 1660s-1690s. He was said to be 80 years old at the time of his death on October 24, 1706.

Original documents from an individual's life, identifying him by name, and authenticated by others, are the best way of knowing anything certain about an historic individual. Such documents have been used in the preparation of this account. However, their limitations as a pathway to knowledge should also be noted. They tend to bring conventional milestones, such as marriage, children, and death, into sharp focus. Moreover, since court records are the most common historical documents that have survived most individual lifetimes, the historian's attention is drawn to extant legal proceedings, which may provide insights into the entire life but rarely represent fairly the whole life. A tempting but often wayward path is for the modern historian to construct a continuous story solely out of available materials or to focus on the available documents as if they alone were significant.

If the original documents provide only an incomplete skeletal framework of an individual's life, the challenge remains: how to flesh out the individual's life so that he appears a living person? The conventional practice of historians since the ancient Greek and Roman authors has been to supply information about the time, place, and society in which the individual lived, as any person is a creature of these circumstances. The careful historian will constantly be checking his own judgment concerning what elements of time, place, and society help create a true and more complete portrait of the individual. But by introducing these elements judiciously, with patience and a careful, plausible application of inference where the facts are incomplete, a rough portrait of a man within his world may be drawn. The biography that follows could perhaps best be described as in the form of a novel, which may be best shortened to "biographical novel," rather than a "novelized" biography, which sounds uncomfortably too novel. (The point to be recognized is that *A Man Named Daniel* is decidedly different from a novel of totally invented characters.)

Finally, beyond the man himself, what may be noted about the society in which he found himself? "Nothing human is alien to me," the Roman comedian, Terence, famously observed. Perhaps. Terence, an African slave in a patrician family who rose above slavery because of unusual talents, may have seen through the whole human comedy to its essence. But for observers of other times, it is probably a better posture to not be too quick to assume that we understand.

What are today's residents of the United States to make of the first English-speaking colonists, who, for example, believed in the reality of witches or the righteousness of slavery or the necessary union of church and state? Encountering these views, actively trying to understand them, may ultimately qualify us also to assert that such a society is not alien to us. But it likely will take many modern readers imagination, sympathy, and some time. Such effort is honest labor.

Final notes concerning documentation

Readers interested in the documentary foundation and structure of *A Man Named Daniel* should consult the substantial bibliography and notes and that follow the main text. The standard elements of scholarship are here, but even more than may be considered standard, the notes provide a discussion in parallel with the story, presenting, at many points, the line of reasoning applied by the author to the sources under consideration. More than just the reasoning alone, the notes also provide confirming or corroborating details of the history that the author, for reasons of storytelling, decided to omit from the narrative.

The notes are organized by chapter and sequentially by page and by the key phrase that is being glossed. No note number appears in the narrative itself, to not disrupt the story with the scholarly apparatus of citation numbering.

The author would be grateful to readers for acquainting him with any additional documentary evidence about Daniel Cone or John Winthrop, Jr., as Daniel's master. Use <u>joccone@mac.com</u> to make contact.

Chronology of *A Man Named Daniel*

Date	Chapter	*A Man Named Daniel*
	Prelude	
April 1630		Lawyer John Winthrop leads 700 Puritans from England; founds Massachusetts Bay Colony.
November 1631		John Winthrop, Jr. (JW2), age 26, arrives in the Colony with second wave of colonists, including other family members.
March 1636		JW2 travels to the mouth of the Connecticut River to found a new settlement, soon named Saybrook.
Winter-Spring 1637		Pequot tribe besieges Saybrook, where Lion Gardiner is in command; colonists retaliate in brutal war against Pequot.
November 1645		JW2 undertakes winter journey to view Tantiusques mine and a potential new settlement at Pequot (New London).
1649		King Charles I beheaded on the orders of Puritan Parliament.
	Chapter 1	
September 1650		Battle of Dunbar; Scots are defeated by Cromwell.

Date	Chapter	*A Man Named Daniel*
September 1651		Battle of Worcester, in which Royalist army, including Scots, led by Charles II, are again defeated by Cromwell; Daniel is captured. Civil War ends; Puritans control England.
November 1651		Merchant ship *John and Sara* departs from London for Boston, carrying Daniel and other Scottish prisoners of war as servants.
	Chapter 2	
February 1652		Daniel arrives in Boston; sold to Richard Leader to work in logging and making charcoal, later in mining (for which charcoal is essential as fuel).
1656?		Daniel becomes servant to JW2, who has close professional relations with Richard Leader.
May 1657		In New Haven, Daniel signs agreement and participates in making charcoal for JW2's mining venture there.
	Chapter 3	
June 1657		Daniel travels to the Tantiusques mine to observe operations for JW2; befriends John Cockrill; meets businessmen John Pynchon and Richard Fellows.
August 1657		JW2 accepts invitation to become governor of Connecticut Colony; Daniel travels to Lynn, meets Mehitable Spencer at the Hammersmith Iron Works farm.

Date	Chapter	*A Man Named Daniel*
May 1662		JW2 obtains royal charter. Daniel marries Mehitable Spencer, daughter of Gerard.
	Afterward	
April 1665		The families of Daniel Cone and Gerard Spencer are among the first settlers of the Thirty Mile Island Plantation (later Haddam).
May 1669		The Connecticut General Assembly confers status of "freeman" on Daniel, allowing him to vote in elections. Daniel is a commissioner for the town.
1683/85		Daniel moves family across river to found new settlement (later East Haddam).
1691		Mehitable dies.
1692		Daniel marries Rebecca, widow of Richard Walkley.
1704		Daniel is one of founding members of First Church of Christ in East Haddam.
1706		Daniel dies at age 80, wills Haddam property to youngest son, Caleb.

Prelude: A New World and a New Venture

The horse breathed heavily as it picked its way along the slippery path. The wind blew the snow hard against the rider's knee stockings, and he stretched his right arm down to pull the cloak around his leg. Shifting the reins he reached down to his other leg, drawing legs and cloak in against the horse's flanks. The horse shivered.

The falling snow kept the riverside path bright, but the traveler knew that the November afternoon was fading. A small clearing on a little slope emerged through the trees.

"Better we should stop now, Thomas," he said. "We shall need the time before dark."

Thomas King directed his mount to a stout tree, dismounted, tied the reins around the trunk, and turned to see if his companion needed him. John Winthrop was already on the ground, too, kneeling. His head was bowed; his horse bent over him against the snow. In a gust, the wind blew the snow off the brim of Winthrop's broad hat, and he opened his eyes and looked up with a little smile.

"It is the day that the Lord hath made, so we shall rejoice in it," he said. "Most especially once He has helped us settle ourselves for this frigid night!"

King needed no further blessing and was already picking up branches from alongside the path. The two men quickly gathered or cut with their axes enough long branches to begin to lash together a shelter, and as King continued with this task, Winthrop hurried to collect more wood for a fire.

Enough of a fire was presently started that Winthrop removed his damp woolen gloves. He rubbed the pale fingers of one hand with the other, minding the fire. So he did not see them approach until the Indians were almost to the clearing.

"Musket!" King called out, seeing the natives in the gathering dusk at the same moment as his companion. [*]

---

[*] Notes to the text begin on page 121.

"No," said Winthrop, coming around the fire, "I think not." He was opening his arms in greeting. He had spotted the man who had befriended them earlier, returning with a group of other men, women, and children.

King put his musket down to his side but watched warily as the Algonkians approached.

"Friend!" said Winthrop, addressing the familiar man and smiling to the others.

"Friends!" he said, motioning them to come closer. None of the Indians spoke, though they continued to come toward the fire, the men first. Two of them held small axes, King saw.

Winthrop focused the full warmth of his smile on the Indian who had helped them earlier that afternoon, returning them to the path from which the Puritans had strayed. The Indian stopped an arm's length before Winthrop and held up his hand. The other Indians stopped. Winthrop watched a scar on the Indian's cheek writhe in the firelight as his mouth moved uncertainly to form a word.

"Frien_!" he said to Winthrop, coming as close as he could to the Englishman's sound. Both men smiled.

The Indian with the scar spoke a few words to his companions, and the women and children came closer to the fire, while one of the men brought forward a rough bag. Winthrop saw that it contained hay for his horse and King's.

"Excellent! Oh, excellent!" Winthrop thanked the man with the hay, who nonetheless held tight to the bag.

The Puritan smiled and looked into a leather satchel he carried over one shoulder. In a moment he produced a small mirror, examined it in the firelight, fogged its surface with his breath, rubbed the surface with his cloak, and held it up for the Indian.

The man recoiled at seeing his face dimly in the shiny glass. The Indian with the scar laughed and took the mirror and gave it to the other. As the hay was still not given to him, Winthrop reached again into his satchel and pulled out a cloth pouch the size of a child's fist. Smiling all the while, he brought the pouch to his nose and inhaled, following this with a look of the greatest contentment.

A single word slowly wreathed from his mouth.

"Tobacco."

The hay then very rapidly found its way into the belly of the Puritans' horses while the smell of fresh tobacco sweetened the air around the fire.

Winthrop stood by the fire and rubbed his hands.

It continued to snow for some hours that night of November 14. After a short time, the natives disappeared back into the forest just as they had appeared. By then, inside their shelter of pine boughs, Winthrop and King had spread out some tall grasses they cut as a buffer against the cold ground and covered that bedding with nets filled with more grass. With the natives gone, John Winthrop lay awake for a time under a woolen blanket, watching the flakes of white fall softly onto the pine branches and needles above his head, and he thought of what had brought him to be lying on the cold ground in this wilderness.

A statue of John Winthrop, Jr., in New London, Conn.

All in all, he must praise God for still being alive. Many with whom he had grown up in England were not, lost in a violently changing world. England was breaking apart, its young men dispersed to colonies or endangered in conflicts. Ever since he was born, the first year of the reign of King James, England had increasingly been split by sharp differences over religious belief, between dissenters and the orthodox Church of England.

What if he had not been born the son of John Winthrop? At quiet moments like this, he liked to reflect on how that fate had shaped his life.

Men like his father, John, believed it their spiritual duty to purify the Church of England of all vestiges of Roman Catholicism and turn it to an austere and strict form of Christianity. After King James, his son, King

3

Charles I, only heightened these Puritans' belief that England was fatally misguided and would be cleansed by God. In preparation for that cleansing, the elder Winthrop became party to a Puritan plan to establish a separate colony across the ocean, and in 1630 Winthrop, chosen governor, led a fleet of eleven ships and 700 passengers to New England, where he became the leader of the Massachusetts Bay Colony.

In only fifteen years, the enterprise had thrived. John watched his

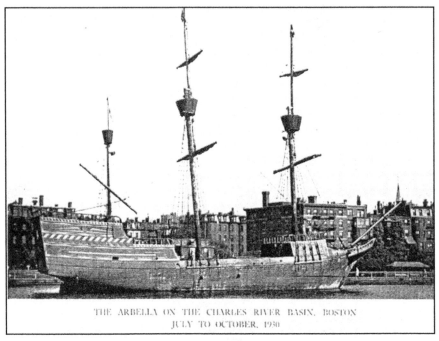

THE ARBELLA ON THE CHARLES RIVER BASIN, BOSTON
JULY TO OCTOBER, 1930

A replica of the ship, Arbella, *that carried John Winthrop and other emigrating Puritans in 1630 was built to commemorate the 300th anniversary.*

father turn all his energies to establishing a model Puritan state. Under his leadership, the Massachusetts Bay Colony established itself through the 1630s and into the 1640s at Boston and in nearby settlements as not only a religious but an emerging commercial enterprise. By the mid-1640s Boston was a city of 1,500 souls and a port of trade with the British West Indies and Europe. The Winthrops did well for themselves financially even as they strove to do good for the Colony—an arrangement that seemed perfectly natural to a country squire turned lawyer turned chairman of a corporation, which legally was what the governor of the Bay Colony was. While his father continued in the colony's governorship or other leadership roles, John served as an elected high magistrate from the year after he arrived, in 1632. And while his father amassed considerable choice acreage in Boston, John, agreeing to establish a defensive outpost for the colony to the north of the city, became a sizable landowner in that new outpost town, named Ipswitch.

As he continued to lie on the cold ground, snowflakes had quite covered the needles above his head, obscuring his view of the heavens above.

What could he have been otherwise?

It was hard to think so emptied. He knew he could have chosen a comparatively more comfortable life, such as name and talent afforded in the Massachusetts Bay. He had shown himself a persuasive advocate of the Puritan mission to the New World from the beginning. He helped administer the provisioning of the Great Migration in 1630; he stayed behind to arrange the sale of his family's country property and shepherd the remaining members across the ocean with additional provisions and settlers. The two ships had left the following year. All this substantial activity was managed in a fashion to not arouse the suspicions of an anti-Puritan king and court. So he knew he could have continued as the adroit operative and indispensable son. But he was restless and needed to be independent.

Bored with Ipswitch, at age 30 he returned to England on the colony's behalf. But he wound up allying himself with another new colonization plan put together by eminent Puritan lords and gentlemen; and he had himself chosen governor of this new colony, which he established at Saybrook, along the shore by a great river to the southwest of Boston. In time he had become less interested in Saybrook, for starting things excited him—but abiding them, not so much. He was not so religious as his father, nor so committed to the prosecution of a religious state. He was drawn to science and commercial enterprises, often to the convergence of the two and particularly to their secret workings. Mining interested him, as did medicine: their inner workings were so unknown.

But what was he doing here this snowy night in November, 1645? His plan seemed clear: Leaving wife and children at home, he was undertaking a winter's journey from Boston to an outpost near the mouth of another river to the southwest, which the Indians called Pequot. There he hoped to consider the possibility of creating another new Puritan settlement, which he would lead. Along the way west from Boston he intended to pass by lands that contained mineral ore that he believed might be rich with what people called "black lead." That substance was used in writing implements and as a pigment. He had set out a surveying party the year before whose collections, assayed in London, seemed promising. Indeed, precious silver was said to be mixed with the black lead deposits. To secure his right to mine the ore, he had purchased the land at Tantiusques from the Algonkian natives.

If the mine was productive and profitable, this would allow him to do . . . *what*, exactly? Where was his life leading?

For a long moment he stared at his canopy of snow and the faint ribs of needles supporting it. No stars shone beyond.

What was . . . since there must be this behind it all . . . what was *God's* plan for him?

"Into Thy hands I entrust myself," said Winthrop softly. With a lingering feeling of uncertainty, he fell asleep.

The next day Winthrop wrote in his journal that the snow "did not melt all that day" as it had on other days. A strong northwest wind blew the snow around, making both staying in place or forging ahead equally difficult. Although the friendly Algonkians sold them venison to eat and offered to "guide us to Tantiusques if we so desired, it seemed better to go on." King and Winthrop reached Springfield the following evening, where a mute testimony to the bitter cold was seen in the Great River, which was frozen. The travelers made directly to the home of William Pynchon, the tiny colony's independent-minded governor. As they approached Pynchon's large cottage, with its barn looming behind it, dogs in a kennel barked loudly. The door swung open just as Winthrop and King reached the threshold, revealing the governor himself.

"Come in, come in, we have been expecting you," he cried, and soon inside, his guests were conducted toward a large fireplace in the middle of a candle-lit parlor. A young couple rose to greet them from chairs by the fire.

"What a pleasure is this, Governor Pynchon?" said Winthrop, in high good humor, his large eyes widening even fuller. "Are we to be greeted by other dignitaries? I believe I see the daughter of a governor of Connecticut? And is that your son?"

"Indeed, sir, it has been some time since we have met," said John Pynchon. "May I present my wife, Amy."

Amy Wyllys Pynchon made the visitors each a small curtsy.

"Honor and cheerful greetings to you both, gentlemen," she said. "Mr. Winthrop, I had the pleasure of meeting you a few years ago at my father's home, but I was still a girl."

"And of course you have changed a great deal," Winthrop replied, "and all most handsomely, I hope I may say. Word had come to me of your wedding last month and your joy in being a bride. Now I can attest with my own eyes that marriage becomes you."

Mrs. Pynchon flushed a little at this gallantry. Her husband beamed.

"My blessings to you both," Winthrop concluded.

Introducing his traveling companion to all, and the two of them taking offered seats near the fire, Winthrop returned his attention to his host.

"We are sorry to arrive so late in the day."

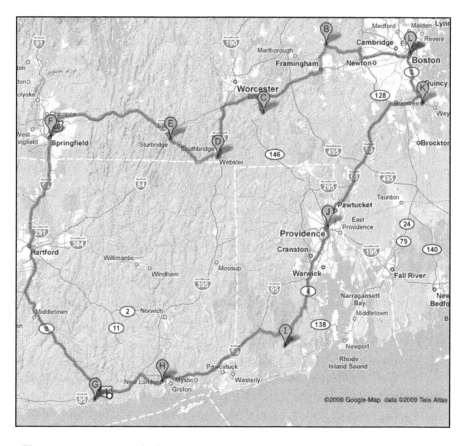

The approximate route of John Winthrop, Jr.'s ambitious winter journey of 1645 is overlaid on a modern road map. He began in Boston and stopped near modern Sudbury [B], Farnumsville [C], Webster [D], Sturbridge [E], Chicopee and Springfield [F] on the first six nights. Tantiusques is just south of [E]. He followed the Connecticut ("Great") River to Saybrook [G]. Pequot [H], the Great Pond [I], Providence [J], and Braintree were other destinations. The trip of over 300 miles took 25 days.

"Do not trouble yourselves about it," said the elder Pynchon. "I am only sorry that Mrs. Pynchon has now gone to bed, as she was very tired and said she felt frightful cold."

"I hope she is not unwell? If I may offer my services?"

"That is kind of you, John, and your knowledge of physic would be most welcome. But I think for now we will put her in the Lord's hands and hope that an early sleep will serve all her needs. Come, tell us of your journey."

Winthrop briefly told of their meeting with the Indians and their failed attempt to reach Tantiusques.

"Where exactly is this place?" John asked.

"You have not told him of this business?"

"It is your venture, and yours to relate," replied the elder Pynchon.

"Fairly spoken," said Winthrop. "But tell me, John, can you keep our confidence?"

"Well, sir, although I am 19," said he, "as you see, I am a sober, married man and, withal, my father's son whose best parts I hope to reflect."

At this speech the three older men chuckled in approval, their humor restrained only by William's ladling out hot cider from a crock by the fire and passing around cups, which all eagerly pressed to their lips.

"So, I shall tell you then," continued Winthrop.

"In 1633—when you were just a lad and still living in Roxbury—a surveying party learned from the Indians about a deposit of ore some 60 miles west southwest of Boston. I heard about it later and put in my mind to do something with it. But as your father well knows, for the last several years my attention on mining has been preoccupied with the Braintree works."

"I am sorry that that enterprise did not end so well for you," the elder Pynchon remarked, after a pause.

"May I ask?" said the young man to Winthrop.

"Well, I will spare your father and wife a story I'm afraid would offer little illumination and perhaps rather too much heat, but I will say this: We started with good intentions, indeed the best of intentions. At Braintree we detected a quantity of iron ore that we thought would yield multiple advantages. First, to our colony, for as you know, we are in need of iron tools—everything from ships' anchors to pins—and it makes much more sense for us to manufacture them ourselves than to procure them from England. Second, because we are fortunate in an abundance which England no longer has—a great supply of trees to make the charcoal to fuel the iron furnaces—we may be able to create valuable exports of iron tools."

As young John absorbed this summary with keen interest, his father pulled a stick from the fire to light his pipe and sat again to puff, awaiting more from Winthrop.

"In addition," Winthrop continued, "–and this has only become more important as hostilities have increased–we hoped for an advantage for our brethren in England, and elsewhere, who might need military weapons."

At the raised eyebrows of young Mrs. Pynchon, Winthrop added, "We pray the Lord to keep us here from conflict of arms. But when our cause is just and the battle joined. . . ." He spread apart his hands and offered a sad smile to Amy Pynchon.

"Finally, as to our venture in Braintree, we hoped for some modest advantage to some few of ourselves, whom God has granted enough to be able to establish ventures of merit."

"What our friend is too modestly not mentioning," said father to son, "is that it was he who took the main risk, of voyaging back to England in 1641, to assemble the group to undertake the project. That could not have been easy."

"As is said, with the Lord all things are . . . well . . . easier," said Winthrop, "and it can be truly said that we have friends whose shared faith overcomes more worldly calculations."

"The Lord looks after his chosen ones," Pynchon said, with a judicious tone.

"I think of good John Becx," continued Winthrop, "a man of our faith but no Englishman–a Dutchman–and when the proposition was put to him of purchasing shares in the venture, he bought forty! In such a way was the company of undertakers of the iron works finally established, two years ago."

"I had heard," Pynchon ventured, "that the company were granted a goodly amount of land in Braintree for the mine operations, and that the General Court granted you these for 21 years."

He paused to inhale on his tobacco, but with a look that he would continue speaking, and presently said, "I also heard that you would be exempt from all taxes–on yourselves, your workmen, and supplies. Is that so?"

He exhaled and added, "I ask not out of envy, but so that young John will learn how such arrangements are made."

"Well, yes. As you know," said Winthrop, "four years ago, the Court passed a law to encourage iron mining and offer some assistance to those taking the risks.

"Mining is a fiendishly difficult undertaking," he continued, directing his observation to the young couple. "So many things may go wrong! Consider we are trying to duplicate the very latest English inventions here in . . . in the wilderness!"

"Indeed," assented the elder Pynchon. "Very difficult, indeed."

He had risen to stand by the fire, and stood poking at and rolling a big log in its center, urging it into the chimney draft. The group's concentration went there, and the less-than-happy conclusion to Winthrop's management of the Braintree works was allowed to slip away with the smoke up the chimney.

"I fear we shall tire our guests if we keep them longer about their stories," Pynchon said to his son, "and I do want to ask about your father," he continued, turning back to Winthrop. "How is my dear friend—other than frightfully busy going about the common good?"

"I shall most gladly tell you about father," said Winthrop, "but I realize I have not answered the question about Tantiusques—and the mine we hope to start there—which your son had wanted."

"I would happily hear that," said Pynchon.

"Well then, last year I purchased the mine and its lands from the Indians," began Winthrop.

"Was that necessary?" interrupted the younger Pynchon.

"A good question. As you know, the Indians are a wandering tribe, or tribes, and don't really own the land, not in our sense. There is no authority that grants them the land, as they are heathens, ignorant of our Lord and of the rights that adhere to Christian kings. Which is why my father, and now our courts, have established in law our rights to all vacant land.

"Even so, I think it wise to establish a record of the establishment of our right to a particular place, especially if it might be valuable or prevent some conflict. At present, for instance, I carry a copy of the deed with me. I'll read you a little of it, John, so you may see how this is done."

Winthrop produced a folded piece of paper from his leather satchel and began to read:

"These are to testifye that I Nodowahunt owner of the land of Tantiusques where the Black lead hill is, Doe sell and give up and surrender all my right in that place for ten miles to John Winthrop the younger—"

" —and it continues for a few more lines, which I won't tire you with. But as you heard, the Indian testified that he gave me all rights to the land—"

"Plainly," said John.

" —and so I dearly wanted to investigate it now, myself."

With an air of finality, Winthrop drained his cup of cider, then added, "but it seems God was not willing at this time."

The assembled group considered the circumstances—the cold, the snow, the Indians, the inscrutable ways of Heaven—and sat thoughtfully, listening to the fire.

"However, let me say this, John," Winthrop resumed. "I shall do more than tell you of this place; I shall see that you are taken there, if you wish, at the earliest opportunity. Will that satisfy your curiosity?"

"Nothing could give me greater interest," said the young man, scarce realizing how prophetic these very words would prove to be.

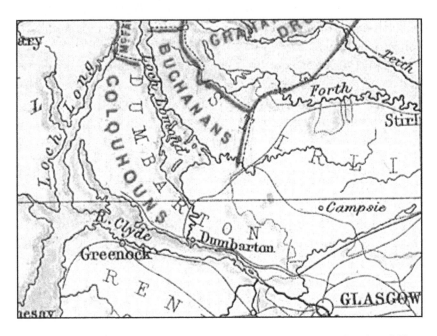

Detail map of Scotland's clans shows Loch Lomond (upper left quadrant) and Clan Colquhoun to its west. The city of Glasgow is southeast, approximately 20 miles from Dumbarton.

Chapter 1. Survivor

A ye, it's him we have to thank!" the man said. But there was no thanks in his voice. The dozen others huddled on the deck laughed without humor, their irons clanking as they moved their legs for warmth in the cold. They stared down at the bulky man on the dock, wrapped in a cloak, talking with the ship's captain.

As they stood together on the deck of the *John and Sara* that chill November morning, the wind cut sharply through their garments of rough wool and linen. An ill-fit lot they were, some with breeches too long, others too short and sleeves likewise, but the clothes were fresh and clean, and for this benefit, at least, the men were in debt to the man on the dock. Problem was, they were indeed in debt to him, as John Becx owned them, every one.

It wasn't only these twelve men but nearly all of the 275 who had boarded the ship two days earlier who were owned by Becx—although "owning" was a bit too broad a term, technically, and not only Becx was involved, as the portly Dutchman was just then reminding the ship's captain below.

"Look ye, Captain Greene," said Becx in strangely accented English, "I know you may not like me, but this is Parliament's work you're doing, you know."

Greene did know; he understood that Parliament, urged by Lord-General Cromwell himself, had ordered that the prisoners of war be deported from England.

"It may be so, sir, but Parliament is not paying me to transport these men," was the Captain's retort. "And you are not paying me."

Becx returned his stare.

"I am to be paid, it says here," said the mariner, pointing to the letter handed him by Becx moments before, "after I deliver your 'servants' to Mr. Thomas Kemble in Massachusetts, where they are to be sold for your 'best advantage and account.' Indeed, sir—"

"Captain!" Becx interrupted, sharp as the sea wind, "you will receive a part of the fee that Mr. Kemble earns as each man is sold. And, as well," he waved off the captain's start to a reply, "you are being paid—in advance—to feed these prisoners during the voyage. Was it not enough?"

"Aye, it is enough—if some of them die."

Becx looked evenly at Greene, who returned a glare.

The hard impasse in the conversation was evident to the men up aboard ship. "Neither a fair wind there, I'd say," said one of them, a man in his twenties.

The thought of a fair wind, of a truly good and wholesome one, brought to his mind a fleeting picture of the breezes that visited his home.

"We're gone away now; we may never see home again," he added quietly, touched by the memory of better times, of his home overlooking that fairest body of water, Loch Lomond.

"Right enough, Daniel," said one of the young man's mates. "And there's an end to it." The voice was bitter.

But was that an end to it? Daniel reflected. Bitter indeed some of the others were. For himself, he had a number of feelings, but bitter was not one of them.

For certain, he had not expected any of this. He would have been much happier if he had never left the lake, never gone from the farm and the cattle he tended up on the hill. He had been tending his own plot and also taking over more of the work from his father, whose heart was weak even though his legs and back were still strong. And so James was not ready to give up all the work on the family farm to his son.

And Daniel—even though he was 25 years old and thought himself ready for any challenge—saw how he must respect this, and they were getting along with it, as if this period of transition were a living person itself, growing into the change. And then the clan decided to throw in its lot with the king, and the men were called.

"You must go. I cannot," James had said, an unspoken grief coloring his face.

So it was, and Daniel accepted this fate and was quietly pleased when the clan made him a dragoon for the wars. It was better to travel by horse, to fight from horse. But the fight itself Daniel was apprehensive about, right from the start.

He had seen King Charles once, before the battle at Worcester, and saw that despite his fancy clothes and the flock of important men hovering around him, he was younger than Daniel himself, and probably no more ready for war.

Charles and the army of Scots were ill prepared indeed for Cromwell and his fighters, which the English called a "new model" army. "New" or not, they were fierce and disciplined— Daniel had seen that in the men who barred the bridge that terrible afternoon. And then the king had fled, and the next thing Daniel knew was that his company of dragoons was surrounded and fired upon by musketeers. The screams of men being hit—

Fighters in Scottish dress reenacting the Battle of Worcester in 2000.

"All men in line!"

Daniel shook at the nearby shout. Leg irons clanked as men moved across the ship's deck. "Head the line aft!" commanded the boatswain.

Daniel took his place in the straggling line of prisoners, a dozen men back from the front of the line, which wound around the stern deck behind the main mast.

Captain Greene stood in an open space before the mast, a hard expression on his leathery face, and waited for the clanking to subside.

"You men! Come one-by-one to the table here and give the clerk your name. He'll write it down in the log, so's we have a record of who's on board. And he'll give you a number. Remember it."

He looked at the ragtag line without any interest. "That is all."

The captain strode away, and Daniel returned to his thoughts as the line began to move.

No, it wasn't what he expected, not at all—a prisoner of war. Still, he was alive. Many who had started with him were not.

Because he knew how to handle a horse and how to be civil to the men who took command, Daniel had better luck of it than many others from Clan Colquhoun who felt pressed into service and showed their feelings.

Many of these clansmen walked, day after day of marching from where they gathered at Sterling, south out of Scotland and into England toward Worcester.

Oh, yes; the war was about the right of the king to rule, rather than the Puritans, and Daniel had no sympathy with these severe Protestants who had killed the young king's father. But he felt no great kinship with the king, despite everyone saying he was of Scottish blood. What had Charles done for Scotland?

"Yours?"

The young clerk looked up from the logbook, annoyed to have to ask and wait.

"Daniel MacCoan."

For a moment the eyes of the two young men held, as the sounds of their voices remained in their minds.

"Daniel" – the Englishman could spell that right enough. But the rest; well, this Scottish tongue trailed off in oo's or o's– but which letters exactly, it was hard to tell.

The clerk, his uncertainty quickly mastered by indifference, wrote down the number 12 and the name "Daniel Mackhoe."

"You're 12," he said to Daniel, but he was already looking at the next man in line.

Daniel stepped to the side under the watchful eye of the first mate of the ship, who sized him up and down, wrote something in a small book, and nodded for Daniel to move along. Daniel walked toward the only clansman he knew who was already done with the line.

"The names are so they can keep us separate, Daniel," John Colquhoun said. "Those of us from the same clan."

"You think they'd know?" Daniel doubted it very much. But there was nothing to be gained from an argument. It would be a hard crossing to New England, and he wanted all the friendly feelings toward him that he could muster.

"Well, all I know," said John, "is that we've suffered a lot already at their hands."

Daniel nodded. The rapid march from Scotland to Worcester exhausted the Scots, especially those who traveled the distance by foot with poor shoes, poor clothing against the nearly constant rain, and poor food. The bread and cheese were often moldy, the beer sour; the Scots wondered just how bad a mistake they were marching into.

Charles believed that his best course was to attack Cromwell, as the old general had been ill ever since his triumph at Dunbar the year before, and the young king believed he would find Royalist supporters in Worcestershire. But until those English supporters materialized, Charles had mainly the Scots to aid him. The Scots' leaders had bargained with Charles to embrace their Presbyterian faith in exchange for naming him king of Scotland. Religion and king made somewhat of a difference to the Scots who followed Charles to Worcester, but of greater interest to the fighting men were support and supplies. These were very slow to arrive.

As the army of 10,000 Scots marched south, the English did not rally to their king. Indeed, besides the uncertain provisioning of food and clothing, the Scots also were short the weapons they needed to confront Cromwell. True, along with their traditional short swords, most had also been given muskets, to stand up better to the muskets of the Puritans. The problem, Daniel knew all too well, was that Charles failed to provide the Scottish musketeers enough ammunition.

He and John and dozens of other men had been helpless on the bridge at Worcester when they had run out of shot to hold off the advancing English. They had held then, waiting for the charge, some of the musketeers holding their guns by the barrel to use as clubs. And the man standing next to Daniel suddenly swung around, his eyes wide as the lead musketball ripped through him, shooting out the backside in a gaping, jagged hole. Then a riot of screaming, men lurching, his horse rearing, Daniel jumping free, grabbing a dropped musket, the crush of men stumbling backward, falling. Of a sudden the cry: Surrender or be killed!

Surrender was not the end of the troubles, though—more like the beginning. That was two long months ago. And yet Daniel did not feel bitter. All in all, he felt fortunate to be alive.

John Colquhoun and Daniel sat quietly on the deck together, absorbed in their own thoughts of the events that brought them to Gravesend while they waited for the others to pass through the line. When that was accomplished, the boatswain spoke.

"You men go below now, as we ready to cast off—except for the ten men I spoke with. Those ten will help above deck."

"And the following men are to report to the cook over there." The boatswain pointed to a heavyset balding man. "You will work in the galley."

The clerk came forward with the first mate's book, with its numbers and checkmarks, compared it to his own list of names, and began calling out numbers and names. Daniel heard his number called and moved toward the heavyset man. As the twelve assembled, the cook looked them over with an expression, thought Daniel, that seemed to betray some amusement, though whether for or against the prisoners he could not tell.

"The galley's fire is big enough to heat four pots: four of you will tend them," the cook said, without preamble. "The galley-room is small, but it's big enough so another four of you will ready the food there for the pots, as I give it over. The last four will serve and clean."

"Any of you had to cook for a big family?"

"Aye!" said Daniel and some other voices. The cook pointed Daniel and three others toward the galley, and Daniel, leg irons rubbing his ankles cold and hard, moved as quickly as he could toward the warmth of that room.

Inside, the room was more than warm; it was hot and dry, the fire eagerly tended by one of the ship's boys. The burning wood of the cookfire was contained inside an open-top box whose sides had holes for air, and the walls of the lead box seemed to pulse with the heat. Daniel eyed the walls of the room, saw that they too were metal and kept them at arm's length. It was never too soon to see where danger lay.

"Ye said y' could cook for a big family," the cook said, following the four Scottish prisoners into the galley. "Well now, what we have on board is like a very big family, y' might say." He smiled. "Except most of 'em don't care at all about you; they just want to be fed."

"Show me, then. Feed 'em!"

With that, he pointed to the four large kettles that stood on a heavy table nearby, turned to his other four helpers and started them chopping onions. That underway, he carved several careful slices off a large ham and began chopping the slices into pieces.

Daniel and his mates saw that beans were soaking in the kettles, so two-by-two they set about lifting the big iron kettles onto large hooks over the fire.

"Does it bother ye?" Daniel asked his older partner, when the man bared a forearm and showed the long deep purple gouge of a swordcut there.

The older man did not reply while they carried the two kettles. But when they were done he spoke softly, just loud enough to be heard above the burning of the wood.

"Dunbar," he said, as if the word spoke volumes.

After the food was served and the galley and cooking-ware cleaned, the cook seemed to ignore the men and left them to themselves. Some went out from the galley, whose temperature was not so much different from outside now that the fire was only embers. Daniel stopped the man with the long scar on his arm, because he sensed some kindness in the older man.

"You mentioned Dunbar," Daniel started, a friendly question in his eyes.

"Well," said he, "the shame of it is that we should have won. We had Cromwell pinned against the sea without a clear way back to England."

"I'd like to hear your story, if you'd care to tell it," said Daniel.

The other sat down on a stool, motioned to Daniel to do the same, and continued.

"So, we had Cromwell pinned. But as I hear it, the ministers ordered General Leslie to move us troops down off the hill, where we had an advantage, and meet the English on the plain. And so we set ourselves up there, one afternoon–a Sunday it was.

"But since it were a Sunday, the ministers wouldn't allow us to fight that day, and so we made camp.

"What happens when you have an animal cornered?" he continued. "Is he more alert, or less alert, I ask you?" The man snorted.

"Cromwell was trapped–but he is no fool, and his blood was up. The next morning while we were still asleep, the English attacked. It was a slaughter."

"I'm so sorry," said Daniel, after a long pause–"I didn't mean to–"

"I lost many friends that day, and to have only the slice here on my arm was a small price. Small price compared to them."

He turned quiet, his face dark. "But that is war, it is."

"Still, you fought again," Daniel observed.

"Aye," said the other. "War is one thing; the treatment after–that should be something else. I canna' forgive the English for how they treated us prisoners.

"I know something of that myself," said Daniel.

"I warrant you do, my lad. I warrant you do. But let me tell you about Chester and Durham, so's you may understand how it is with me."

One side of his face was dimly illuminated by the ember-light, and that eye took on a fierce redness that held Daniel in its gaze.

"Just now, after Worcester, I was imprisoned at Chester," he continued. "Many, many good men died, of their wounds, or of disease. Me, I was released–that's part of another story, not for now. And again we were marched, in only scraps of clothing, not enough to shield us from the cold, barely enough to cover our nakedness–no better than dogs."

He stared beyond Daniel to across the room and drew his next breath deeply.

"Men with me were marched in their bed clothes—true as I stand here! Everyone was starving. Myself, I ate only some peas that I pulled out of a field when no one was looking. And the English folk along the march, some yelled at us and threw sticks and rocks. It was disgusting, not fit . . . not fit *at all*—for the dignity of a man."

He lowered his eyes and shook his head.

"And yet, for all that, it was not worse than Durham, the cathedral there, where I was imprisoned after Dunbar—and after such a march that I have no stomach at all to speak of now."

He paused again and wiped his eyes with the back of his hand.

"Of Durham, the less said the better, but I shall tell you this, that made me want to kill *all* Englishmen. We were kept like beasts—worse than beasts—inside the cathedral. No fuel against the cold. Little food—and here was the Devil in them—little food except what we could get from ransoming off to our guards whatever poor possessions we still had.

"When men had no more, and the flux had taken hold of them and their bowels, many a man would do things he would never have done otherwise to another Scotsman just to get food. And can ye blame them? Nay, I can not. I blame the English—the murderers!

"And that has put me here, I suppose."

He came to an abrupt end. His eyes were cast down, and he raised first one hand and then the other, together rubbing his forehead.

Daniel studied the other's face in the flickering shadows. After a long moment, he thought of nothing to ease the other's pain and would not say something false.

But it was with a kindly voice that Daniel spoke next.

"Let us go out and get some rest."

The other nodded. "My name is Ewan Taylor, by the bye," he said.

Outside, it was long since dark. A pale blade of a moon shone cold in the sky as Daniel and Ewan made their way quickly across the deck of the *John and Sara*.

Daniel stole a glance from the moon to its broken reflections in the dark waves as the deck dipped and lifted, and it made him uneasy in the pit of his stomach. He had never before been on a ship at sea.

He grasped the handrail inside the door that led to the ladder below decks. He heard voices from below, a loud one that stuck out and then a sharp louder one that struck back, and he turned to look at Ewan. The other's face was dark and troubled, as if recalling the prisons. And it struck Daniel all at once: He was alone again in larger worlds that might bear him no good—three hundred captive men; the cold hazards of winter; the great dark rolling otherworld of the sea.

What lay in store for him, and for them all? He could not know, but he clenched his teeth and spoke to himself.

"I will survive!"

Chapter 2. New England, Old Servitude

D aniel waited, again. It was not so bad as a change. The march had been hard.

He heard that some men had died, even though it had not been that long. The Scots had arrived yesterday morning in Boston, and now it was afternoon. The march had been through snow, and the biting cold had pierced through their poor garments. Again.

But Daniel felt it was not so bad. He had stepped off the ship's gangplank onto the ground and fell to his knees.

"God be praised," he'd said, and leaned over, kissing the rough plank of the wharf.

"*God be praised!*" he'd said again softly, tears welling up in his eyes. Solid ground. Not the vast uncertainty of the sea.

"You there, get up!"

He'd heard the voice and felt the stamping on the plank toward him, and he'd moved to rise, but his legs felt like uneven metal springs, and he stumbled as he stood, his sense of balance queer and amiss.

"Stay in line. Understand?" The man brandished a musket and an impatient glance, and left as soon as he saw Daniel upright and moving forward.

Snow was falling lightly as the line of men left the *John and Sara.* It must have been snowing for some time that February morning, as the wharf and the main street connecting it to the town were now covered in a fine powder. White and clean, he had thought. Fresh.

Turning over in his mind this thought of freshness made standing in line again pass more agreeably for Daniel, and before long he had joined the growing group of other men who were gathered into a large barn at the head of the dock, waiting. The Scots were from many clans, including Grant, Ross, and Stewart, as well as Colquhoun.

Some had started the voyage were not there. He had been on deck often enough with the others, silent, as another dead man, laid out in the clothes he had died in, was given a curt farewell by the captain, then slid on a board over the side and into the sea. Daniel had not realized how many dead there were. He had been told by the ship's cook, who'd seemed to know just about everything that happened on board, that 28 Scots had died during the voyage, about one out of every ten of them that began.

Some had finally died of their wounds from Worcester or from the wretched imprisonment which followed; and some were so weakened with the constant cold, the near-constant violence of the sea, the poor food, and the crowded, filthy conditions with scores of other ill and wretched men, that they had stopped struggling and slipped under this hostile surge. And then a few indeed had literally fallen over the edge, losing their lives while working on deck or in the sails' rigging during one winter storm or another.

Those who survived were mainly the stronger, the younger, and the luckier, and as they had waited in the barn, none looked back on the *John and Sara*, tied up in the cove, with other than cold eyes.

When the orders had come for most of them to form a single line and march, they walked away from the sea, into the town of Boston. Once away from the wharf, they passed only a few other souls on the street, just a few hardy men who darted in and out of a group of small shacks in some kind of marketplace.

Smoke wreathed out a chimney of the largest of the shacks; pigs and a few chickens in cages stood outside in the cold. The man in front of him in line turned around, pointing

The road leading from Boston harbor to Lynn past the Winthrops' house (identified with arrows) is shown in this reconstructed period map.

with his head across the street. Daniel saw the familiar shapes of stocks and pillories, their beams outlined in snow.

The Scots were marched somewhere to the north, to a place the English called Lynn. Men cried out over their leaking shoes and the blisters and bleeding they caused. The blood tracked the line of march in red.

They stopped while it was dark, ate a cornmeal mush, drank cider, and slept poorly, in another barn, and started again at dawn, going as far as a river, named Saugus. Daniel was among those near the front of the line who were ferried across. As ferrying took time, more of the men were marched to a bridge and crossed the river there. Once together they were stopped again.

This time the waiting was different, because they all understood what was next. That man Becx, back in London, had bought them, and now they were going to be sold.

John, Daniel's kinsman, had said that another Scot learned that Becx had paid five or six pounds each for the Scots but that the going price in New England was 20 to 30 pounds. That's what was paid for the Scots captured at Dunbar, people said. And Becx had some of them sent to the businesses he had major interests in—an ironworks here where they stopped and a group of sawmills farther north, including a place called the "Great Works."

Daniel didn't like it at all that Becx was going to make money over selling him and his mates, but the profit wasn't the main thing that bothered him. It was the freedom, the loss of it. For six or seven years more, or maybe eight, he would be a servant with very few rights.

And so the Scots looked closely at the English who had clustered around the man named Kemble (or Campbell, some of the Scots said— although it was probably not Campbell, thought Daniel). The men were saying that Kemble had connections to sawmills and to logging, and so maybe they wouldn't work at the ironworks after all, but in the forests.

Among those talking with Kemble was a man to whom the others gave some deference—more than that, just a bit of distance. They knew Richard Leader as a capable man, an engineer, who the Undertakers of the Iron Mines had hired to replace John Winthrop, Jr., back in 1645. And lead, Leader had surely done. He moved the base of the ironworks operation from south of Boston, at Braintree, to north, along the river that had the Indian name, Saugus. He had gained experience in iron mining in England, and he supervised construction of a blast furnace, a forge, and a slitting mill along the river. The Hammersmith Ironworks looked to be a success, and Leader became one of a handful of most influential and best-paid men in the Bay Colony.

And then some conflict arose, and the normally even-tempered Leader publicly criticized the Colony's Governor Endecott, the Colony's court of magistrates, and even the Church. The other men couldn't remember two years later entirely what the dispute had been about, but the Court imposed a harsh fine against Leader–200 pounds–and that wasn't something you forgot. As it happened, Leader apologized, the fine was reduced, and then the next thing, he was gone. He left Lynn and went to the Undertakers' sawmills up north.

Now he was back, just as he had been a year earlier, when the Scots from Dunbar arrived to be sold. Leader had taken twenty of them then, and the other Englishmen standing nearby assumed that Becx had gotten word to him that there were more new Scots to be had.

Leader took advantage of the distance his peers gave him to walk up and down before the ragged Scots.

"You men have had it hard," he said, pausing before the group.

"War." He watched their faces.

"Prison." He saw blank or defiant expressions.

"A devil of an ocean, am I right?" He offered them a knowing smile, and a few hearty Scots shouted back, "Aye!"

"And I bet you're sick of the salt pork, the pea soup, the cold porridge every day at sea." Again, some nodding heads.

"So here's my proposition to you, and I'll speak you true: If you're not afraid of hard work . . . if you're ready to make a new life here, I will help you. Yes, you'll work for me–and yes, it'll be seven years. But I will see to it that you are treated well, clothed and fed well, and fairly given a chance to improve yourself, according to your work."

Leader paused to see what effect he was having. Their faces showed that many of the Scots paid him close attention.

"Aye, I will take an interest in you. And *why?*

"I will tell you. This land needs men who are ready and able to look forward, not back. To grow; not shrivel and die–despite whatever hardships you have endured. It is in *my* interest to bind such men to me."

The undercurrent of conversations in the room, among both the Scottish prisoners and their prospective masters, had broken up as Leader spoke. The room was hushed.

"These gentlemen behind me," he continued, "could vouch that I tell the truth even when others don't agree or when it seems not to my advantage to speak so. I invite any of them to speak, and say I am not as I have said . . . and will *not* do as I say."

The cluster of English gentlemen around Kemble said nothing but looked rather sheepish. With a smile, Leader turned back to the Scots.

"Now, who among you wishes to be considered, step forward. I will choose twenty of you."

From his place in this midst of the Scots, Daniel quickly stepped forward in front of Leader.

As Kemble, Leader and the other Englishmen knew well, Daniel and the other Scots prisoners of war had few formal rights. In fact, they could be sold as slaves, as the godly Puritans had set out in their "Body of Liberties" a decade before. The Bay Colony codified their complicated view of slavery in a law that drew its authority from the Bible:

> There shall never be any bond slavery amongst us, unless it be lawfull captives taken in just warrs, and such strangers as willingly sell themselves, or are solde to us.

As the Puritans considered the Scots "lawfull captives taken in just warrs," the prisoners' ultimate day of freedom would be decided by their owners. Freedom would come, though, at least according to what the Colony's Reverend John Cotton had told Oliver Cromwell about the Scots captured at Dunbar: "They have not been sold for slaves to perpetual servitude, but for 6 or 7 or 8 years. . . ."

Other slaves, black slaves, were a different story. Black Africans had been sold in Boston since the mid-1630s, obtained during voyages from England that stopped in Africa, the West Indies, and Boston. And their servitude could be without end, as the Bible supported:

> Of the children of the strangers that do sojourn among you, of them shall ye buy, and of their families, and they shall be your possession. They shall be your bondsmen forever.

How these Puritans, who felt themselves aggrieved against the authority of king and his church, could so readily turn about and act the grievous authority against other outsiders is a question that perhaps few of them reflected upon. But as the brother-in-law of John Winthrop, Sr., expressed it to him in 1645, the motive for buying "Moores"—blacks—as slaves was at least partly economic:

> I doe not see how wee can thrive until wee get into a stock of slaves sufficient to do all our business . . . and I suppose you know verie

well how wee shall mayneteyne 20 Moores cheaper than one
Englishe servant.

John Winthrop, Jr., looked out the window at Theophilus Eaton, as
he departed down the path, attended by his African slave.

Eaton was a man to be reckoned with. He knew that from years ago,
when Eaton and the Reverend John Davenport had arrived in Boston with
their Puritan followers, a particularly well-to-do group that had impressed
even his father. Davenport and Eaton had moved their flock to New Haven
twenty years ago, and it must be admitted, as Winthrop's wife was fond of
telling him, that the city was prospering. Just look, she would say, at the
many fine homes arrayed around the Green.

Eaton was the governor of that prosperity; Winthrop nodded as he
thought the phrase. Indeed, Eaton was the elected governor of the New
Haven colony, and had been so for more than a decade, re-elected repeatedly
by the other town fathers who recognized that he was an astute businessman.
After all, years ago, hadn't it been Eaton who had served King Charles as a
commercial agent in Denmark, even though he was a Puritan? His ventures
benefited many of the New Haven men, even while making himself the
wealthiest in the colony.

Eaton was used to having his views followed. Oh, he was civil about
his complaints to Winthrop, but rigid, finally. Rigid, and too severe, these
men of New Haven were, as a lot. Observing the Sabbath strictly—of course
that was right, but were the Sabbath prohibitions on cooking, bedmaking . . .
even kissing your own children? What did they add? Why were they needed?

Winthrop sighed in his empty parlor, continuing to watch the path,
though Eaton was no longer visible.

The investors in the mine were "men of God, first and last," Eaton
had said, and they were "alarmed—Nay, Mr. Winthrop—aghast," at the
behavior of some of the workmen that had been brought to work in the iron
bogs to the east of New Haven. Drunkenness, swearing, Sabbath-breaking,
depravity of "the worst sort," Eaton said. "We place our trust in you to
govern them more strictly."

Pinion. Well, it was true, or at least he had heard most of it before,
about Nicholas Pinion. He and his wife had been in and out of court in
Massachusetts over the worst sorts of offenses. Beating his wife. Causing a

miscarriage, it was said. And the wife, Ester, no lady herself but beating him on many occasions with her fists and feet, and openly carrying on with another man. And drunkenness many times, and that scar on his head where Nicholas was cracked by an iron staff. Many trips to court.

And so it went.

But that seemed to have been mostly finished with 10 years ago. Yes, it was true that he had kept Pinion out of the stocks, as Eaton well knew. But the man could be reformed. He was hard-working, determined, and ingenious, in his own way. The discipline he showed in his work could be brought into the rest of his life.

Winthrop wrinkled his long nose and snorted. The Lord knew that he hadn't agreed with everything his father said, but he kept in his heart some words from the speech on Christian charity that John Winthrop had given to his fellow Puritans at sea on their way to New England, 25 years earlier. Thinking of Eaton and of Pinion, he spoke the sentence to himself:

> Wee must delight in eache other, make other's conditions our owne, rejoyce together, mourne together, labour and suffer together, allwayes haveing before our eyes our Commission and Community in the worke, our Community as members of the same body.

Well, Winthrop thought, those are fine ideals to strive for, as sound today as anytime. He wrinkled his nose again.

Anyway, he needed Pinion to make the mine work. Leader had said he was among the best, and would help make a success of it. And Eaton and the others certainly wanted the ironworks to succeed. That's what he emphasized to Eaton, and the man seemed mollified, if not content.

It's what *he* personally wanted in New Haven.

Eaton and Davenport had courted him, and lured him with this fine house and the share in the ironworks. It had been hard to leave what he had built in New London. He liked the world he made there rather better than the suspicious and rather inflated way of these New Haveners. He would see how the mining progressed this year. But he remembered the friendly overtures to him from Roger Williams in Rhode Island, the men in Hartford, and even the Dutchman, Peter Stuyvesant, in New Amsterdam.

Who could say for sure where he would be living in 1658? That was next year. For now he needed to show what iron could be made here. If Eaton was feeling some impatience, so was he!

More than 27 years ago, before he had even left England, his father had said that iron was going to be the gold of New England. And now nearing 50 years old himself, he felt that he must make a success of this. While others had profited from mining, although he had tried, as yet he had not.

As Winthrop continued to stare out the window at this path, he spied three men approaching from some distance, and his thoughts moved to the present.

Yes, Richard Leader was an able man, and he did not mind being in his debt, Winthrop reflected. Leader had the sawmills and still had the connections at Lynn, and he had been able to tell him about men that were worth having with him, if the New Haven venture was to succeed.

Winthrop had to smile, remembering it. He had borrowed a saddle from Leader, ten years before, when Leader had invited him to visit Braintree, and his own saddle strap had broken. Here was Leader again, helping him again into the saddle. Winthrop was particularly happy for his recommendations when it came to servants. Winthrop considered himself a good judge of character, and he had had many opportunities over two decades time to test that judgment against individuals who were presented as potential servants. One's judgment might be good, but a second, confirming judgment was even better. Thus he valued Leader.

So many elements, so many humors, so many unknowns —on the one hand, it was the sort of problem Winthrop enjoyed in a medical diagnosis. On the other, the servants were so unpredictable, particularly the prisoners. They might start out well enough, but then . . . like that fellow, Salmon, whom he had let go two years before.

In fairness, the Scots had a grievance; many had been badly used by them. But some, like this Daniel, had decided to let the past go and make the best of the present.

John Winthrop, Jr. (a.k.a. "the Younger")

The three men arrived at the door and knocked. Winthrop gave up his musing and moved to open it.

"Mr. Winthrop, I've come," cried the stocky fellow in front, with a strange intensity.

"Goodman Cotter, please enter," said Winthrop in a hearty voice, adding, "I'm glad to see all three of you together – that way we may resolve our little business as swiftly as possible." And Winthrop nodded to the other two men as they, too, entered the parlor.

Taking his seat behind a simple but well-made writing desk, Winthrop offered the seat opposite to Cotter. The two other men continued to stand, to the back.

Cotter sat down heavily in the chair, resting his hands at first along its arms, and then, noticing that the sides of his thumbs had black smudges on them, he put his hands to unaccustomed rest in his lap. Winthrop watched him and waited, an easy smile curving his moustache.

"As you know," began Cotter, "I've bound myself to pay you in coal to complete our agreement for Eleanor Sartell."

"Her services are meeting your needs, I take it?"

"Oh, yes," he replied slowly. "There's some who'd told me to beware these Irishwomen as servants, as they are too wild and free. But that don't bother me." With the back of his hand he rubbed his chin with its goat's beard.

"Anyways," he continued, "I trusted more what you told me of Eleanor when she worked for you. She is good to my little girl. And she's a help to me, she is."

"I am very glad that she has made the change to your home agreeably," offered Winthrop.

The other looked across the polished desk at Winthrop and grunted.

"Yes, so now I'd like to conclude with you."

Turning about in his chair, Cotter continued, "If either of these Scotchmen will cut enough wood for me, I shall make a quantity of charcoal equal to what I still owe you for Eleanor."

"That was ten pounds in money, I believe we agreed," said Winthrop. "How much would that be in coal?"

Cotter cleared his throat.

"I think it fair if you gave me the same price for this coaling as is allowed to the others who coal the wood for the ironworks," he replied.

"Fair indeed," replied Winthrop, "supposing that you will yield about the same amount of charcoal from my wood as do the others."

Cotter grunted again and took his time in replying while he surveyed the wall behind Winthrop, with its books and papers. "I should think I do— at the very least," he said in a harder voice.

"Of course you will," said Winthrop, noticing. "And so I shall leave the weight to you."

Changing his focus to the men behind Cotter, he added, "It's possible I might need Daniel for other work before he finishes with you. I think that's not likely, as he's an experienced and quick man with an axe and saw—learned up at the Great Works, you know."

"Yes, Daniel's told me some of his work up north. Some day I'd like to see the country there myself. And I know he's had some experience in making coal—Daniel has." He paused, scratching the side of his head, as if to stimulate a thought that would give him an advantage. After a moment he spoke again.

"But for this coaling, I intend to do it all myself, as it's my debt," said Cotter, and turning around to Daniel added, "meaning no offense to you."

"No offense taken; none at all," said Daniel, mildly.

"Good then, it sounds as if we have a clear understanding," said Winthrop. "If you give me just a moment, I will write it down, Goodman Cotter, so that we have a record of our agreement."

Winthrop drew a sheet of smooth paper from the drawer in his desk, and with rapid flourishes of his quill pen distilled what had been said. Cotter followed the feather tip of the quill as it danced in the air to the shaping of the letters, and he thought how interesting it was that he, a working man who could not read or write, would have gained the notice of Mr. Winthrop, a friend of Governor Eaton and the Reverend Davenport and of many other worthy men, mainly because he knew the business of charcoal-making so well.

"There," said Winthrop, putting down the quill. "Done." He smiled at Cotter.

"Sometimes I can't even read my own hand-writing, so with your permission I'll just read this aloud, so we may all hear it together, and then you may sign, and Daniel and John may witness."

"'These are to testify that I, William Cotter,'" began Winthrop, and the mention of his own name so soon caught Cotter's attention and caused him to listen carefully to the rest of it, as it rolled out in one long sentence.

"You've captured just what we said," said Cotter with a note of admiration in his voice that surprised himself a little.

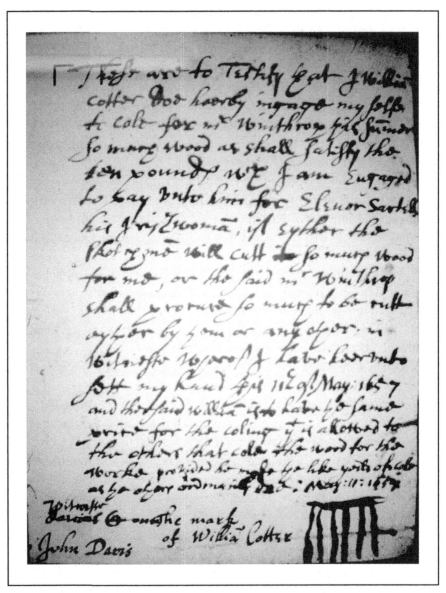

This is the earliest known document with Daniel's name and signature. The microfilm reproduction of the May 11, 1657 agreement between John Winthrop, Jr., and collier William Cotter shows Cotter's mark in the lower right and the signature of "Danial Con[n]" squeezed in at the left, as a witness. (In the seventeenth century, spelling was often done phonetically, with frequent inconsistency between writers.)

"So, if you'd be so kind as to sign it here, then," said Winthrop, "and then the others."

Cotter took up the quill and dipped it into the ink, dribbling it a bit as he brought it across the paper, unaccustomed as he was to handling such an instrument. He made one broad stroke across the bottom corner of the page, and then drew six lines down from the first, as far as the edge of the page.

"There!" he said, looking at his signature. "Logs stacked for coaling."

Cotter passed the pen to the nearer man, who quickly wrote, "John Davis," and passed the pen to Daniel.

Daniel came up to the edge of the table and dipped the quill into the inkwell again, but having observed the fate of Cotter's excess ink, he lightly tapped the quill, as he had seen Winthrop do, and quickly took the pen to paper.

"Danial," he wrote, in the spelling that seemed right to him. He paused. There was a nice solidity to his writing, as thick and manly as Cotter's mark. He dipped the quill again, for more ink, and delayed again.

He *was* proud to be a Scot—the Lord knew that he was, and besides, everyone who cared to know, knew that he was, too. But he had decided that there was no need to emphasize it. This wasn't Scotland anymore, and he had a hard time imagining how he would ever see the country of his birth again. . . . New England was his home now, and he was determined to make the most of whatever it had to offer him. So he had made up his mind when he worked for Mr. Leader to drop the "Mac" from before the rest of his name.

He put pen to paper, emphasizing the "C" in a neat thick coil. He paused to examine it, then drew the letters that made the sound he thought of as his name, "–onn." "Conn," he had written. Like the seed pods in the giant evergreen trees, he said to himself. He liked that association.

He put the quill down on the desk. Winthrop picked it up and wrote something quickly.

"I have added the day's date, May 11, 1657," said Winthrop.

"And so we have an agreement, Mr. Cotter. These men may begin to supply you the wood as soon as you're ready."

"I'm ready now; they can begin today," he said, then added, "by your leave."

Winthrop smiled and nodded his assent.

Cotter rose from his chair, keeping his smudgy hands to himself. With a quick bow, he departed Winthrop's parlor, John and Daniel following him out.

This was the part Daniel found fascinating. Everything about producing charcoal had its challenge, that was for sure. Some of those tall oaks that he and John had chopped down that month—well, a man placed his cuts carefully into the trunk, but a tree sometime seemed to have a mind of its own about where it wanted to fall, wasn't that so? They used their experience and for the most part, they had been lucky, he and John, but he'd just as soon forget about those two oaks—especially the one that had snapped back right toward John. It was the hand of God, only, that kept John from being killed.

For two weeks the two of them had sawn the logs. Every day but the Sabbath, the two of them to either side of a big two-handed saw, one log after the other. The challenge then wasn't in knowing how to fell the oak; it was the strength and persistence in cutting up the hard, green wood.

This is the earliest known signature of Daniel (see p. 32 for context)

This morning William Cotter had plunged into the day's work early, working a cleared spot in the field not far from the log stacks. He had driven a stake into the ground, dropped a ring over the stake, tied a rope to the ring, and marked out a circle on the ground by walking around the stake at the full length of the rope. He had traced a circle about four times a man's height across and then fell like a fiend to hacking and digging into the soil. He called to John and Daniel, "Give it all you got, men. Break your backs! Tonight you will sleep like a log!" And he had laughed hard at his own humor, as he always did.

But they liked him and they had set to it with a will, and by noon they had the ground cleared, a shallow pit dug, and soil, leaves, and other debris put at the edges of the fire ring. Then they had moved the logs, wheelbarrow by wheelbarrow, from the stacks over to the ring. Although Daniel had seen it done many times at Lynn, and helped out close enough that he knew he could do it if needed, Cotter insisted on building "his pyramid" of logs all by himself.

Every piece of just the right size he placed on its side, or on its end, evenly all the way around, building up the structure piece by piece, just so. After hours of hard work and many oaths (it were well that Mr. Winthrop had not heard), Cotter had his pyramid, nearly twice a man's height in the center and sloping fairly evenly all the way around. He walked about the pyramid once, then twice, talking to himself and poking the pile here and there, trying to see if the stacks were loose or unsteady anywhere.

"An unstable stack is the Devil's work," he called out from the side opposite where Daniel and John stood waiting. "*The Devil's work*!" he repeated, as they came into view of him. "An unstable stack falls and creates a burning fire, like Hell!"

And he laughed again, although this time it was clear he did not think a burning fire was funny; and Daniel knew the biggest challenge in charcoal-making was to keep the fire low so the wood only charred, and avoid a roaring fire, which burned everything to ash.

They shoveled up the grass, soil, roots, and other debris that they had dug to clear the fire ring and the pit, and all three of them heaved it onto the lattice work of logs. It covered about half the pyramid, and to cover the rest William had Eleanor, his servant, bring up a wagon which contained more grass, and stalks, and roots. Over much of this he applied a thin layer of mud, which he mixed from soil and water in a trough that Eleanor had also brought.

Finally, Daniel and John sat on the ground, arms and legs sore. Daniel watched as Cotter stalked about the covered pyramid, with a long stick opening an airhole here and there by some exact reasoning that only he seemed to know but about which he appeared completely confident. The placement and size of the holes were critical, and these first holes were only the beginning. Later Cotter would need to close holes or open others to control the fire and the charring of the wood inside.

But for this day, there was only one more step. Cotter placed a curved ladder gingerly against the pyramid, and with one hand held a forked pole that supported him off the pile while with the other hand he carried an iron box that he kept away from his body and away from the pile. At the top of the pile, he looked down the opening that he had created around the center, and satisfied that the opening went all the way to the ground, he carefully opened the iron box and poured out several handfuls of brightly glowing coals.

"That should start her!" he cried. On the ground, Eleanor, John, and Daniel clapped their hands heartily. Cotter clambered down the ladder, but did not join in the applause. He waited for the first whisps of blue smoke to come out the top-hole.

When they came, he did not cheer. The pyramid would char for five or six days and during all of it, he knew he would need to remain vigilant, morning and night, since a flaw in the burning left untended could at any time ruin the whole and all their work.

Daniel leaned over the bucket and splashed water up onto his face and chest. It was good to be back in New Haven, now that the colliering was done. He felt good that Goodman Cotter had asked him to sit up with him the night before, to mind the fire for some hours so that he might get a little sleep.

He grabbed the towel on the hook next to the pump and dried himself off. He had earned a little extra money for that nighttime labor. A man, and especially a servant, needed to do what he could to make his way in the world. Daniel quickly pulled his shirt on over his head, shook out his long hair, and brushed away two little twigs that had stuck onto his leggings. He was ready to see Mr. Winthrop.

As he strode past the barn, he heard the stable boy murmuring softly to the mare Daniel had ridden back from the woods. The evening air was beginning to lose the weight of the sun, and Daniel walked with a lighter gait, eager to hear what his master wanted with him.

From the parlor door, Daniel heard Mr. Winthrop's voice bidding him enter, and soon he was seated in the desk chair opposite Winthrop, telling him that the charcoal-making had gone well and that, he thought, Cotter's obligations would be met.

"This pleases me, Daniel. You have done well. Now I need you do something else for me."

"Only say it and it will be done," said Daniel.

Winthrop sat back, considering the man. Always ready but not servile. Confident. How it touched him to consider this Daniel, young

This idealized vision of the steps of making charcoal (see letters A-F in illustration) is from eighteenth century France.

enough to be his son, in comparison to his own sons, weak and unsure as they were.

"I know," Winthrop replied, after a long pause. "I have confidence in you." He smiled at the younger man.

"Which is why I am charging you with some delicate business for me. I want you to carry a letter to John Pynchon in Springfield. He is engaged with me in another mining operation at a place called Tantiusques. I will ask him to have you guided there."

"What do you want me to do there?"

"This is where the delicacy is, Daniel." Winthrop had taken up his quill pen, and was balancing its point against his little finger.

"The operation there goes slowly—and not well," he resumed. "There are difficulties, I am sure of it, but whether it be in the conditions of the mining, or the men who are engaged, or some mixture of these, I can not say from a distance. And I fear that if I were to involve myself too directly, I would not receive a normal view, of how things truly are."

Winthrop paused to study if the other man understood the nuances. Alert he was, this Daniel. He had survived Worcester, and Winthrop remembered what his uncle had written—that Lord-General Cromwell himself had said that at Worcester "there were four hours as hard dispute as ever he met with." Cromwell was no man to exaggerate, and this Daniel had survived the battle and hardships since. Perhaps this was a sign of God's favor.

"Furthermore," Winthrop continued in a more animated tone, "Mr. Pynchon might take my presence amiss, as an affront to his judgment or management, which I certainly, you understand, do not intend – and which, under no circumstances, are you to even hint at. Besides, I have other business which must shortly take me to Hartford."

"I understand, Mr. Winthrop," said Daniel. "I am to visit the mine, observe activities there closely, talk with the workers, but cause no particular attention to be drawn to my presence or your interests."

"Precisely," said Winthrop. "I shall take the report of what you have seen and heard directly from you, when we have both returned. There is no one else with whom you should discuss this purpose or your observations. Am I clear?"

"Completely clear," said Daniel.

"Unless you have a message from me while you are at Tantiusques, stay there and work for one week and then return. That should provide ample time to observe the true state of the business. When you return here, you will resume with Goodman Cotter."

As was his habit, he rose to signal the coming end of the discussion.

"I'll ask you also to deliver some medicines for Mrs. Pynchon."

"I am sorry if she is not well," said Daniel, rising. He had been told by other servants that Amy Pynchon had spent more than a year in Mr. Winthrop's care, at the Winthrop home.

"But I've heard how well she trusts your help, Mr. Winthrop."

Again, nothing servile in the remark; just a quiet confidence, thought Winthrop.

"And I yours," he said.

Daniel smiled.

As he left the house, the sun was just setting behind West Rock, turning the sky a soft pink. Two boys were walking away from the Green with their father in the evening stillness. Daniel quickened his pace, suddenly eager to catch . . . something—he knew not what.

Chapter 3. The Governor's Trust

All along the Connecticut River Daniel followed the road north from Hartford, and the river was a steady companion, albeit going in the opposite direction from his own. When he stopped the horse to drink, this hot June day, he took a little extra time to remove his stockings and cool his own feet in the river.

The Wyllys family had given him letters for Amy and told him that he should have no trouble spotting the Pynchon house and farm at Springfield, as it was the one best situated near the river on the eastern shore. Indeed it was a fine house, thought Daniel, as he approached, though rather different in its isolation from the way Mr. Winthrop lived in New Haven. The Wyllyses said the house had been built by William, the father of Amy's husband, before he returned to England.

He had heard just a little of William Pynchon and knew that he had been a successful merchant, a great trader in furs with the Indians, and quite independent in his thinking— somewhat too independent, it seemed, because a religious book he wrote put him in grave trouble with the Colony, and Daniel heard he left New England to return to Cromwell's England because of it. So all in all it

The Pynchon house and farm at Springfield

didn't surprise Daniel that the Pynchon estate was in a prominent perch and also rather separated from others. A serving woman spotted him as he rode up the path alongside the master's house, and she brought him inside to wait for John Pynchon. As he surveyed the room Daniel saw signs of wealth that were new to him. In the corner stood a glass-front cabinet, richly carved in a dark reddish wood that he was sure he had never seen before—not in Mr. Leader's home nor in Mr. Winthrop's. He went closer to inspect it.

"You've brought a letter for me?"

Daniel turned around to see a man about his age with a mild and curious expression.

"Yes, sir, three letters, in fact—if I am speaking with Mr. Pynchon."

John Pynchon's expression broadened. "You are, and who are you?"

"I am Mr. Winthrop's man, Daniel Cone."

"Well, Daniel, I will be obliged to you for delivering the three letters to me. Thrice obliged, I should say," and he smiled at his own small witticism.

Out of a small bag, Daniel gave Pynchon the letters for his wife from her mother and brother, and the letter for him from Winthrop.

"Mr. Winthrop instructed me to ask you that I be brought to the lead mine," Daniel said as he gave over the Winthrop letter. "I think this letter is about that."

"He also gave me some medicines—for your wife, I believe," said Daniel and handed over a small package which gave off a subtle, complex aroma of many herbs.

"Oh, this is most welcome!" exclaimed Pynchon, and he brought the package up to his nose and smelled it.

"I shall see that you are brought to the mine tomorrow," he said, placing the package carefully onto a side-table. "And now, since you've brought good things to us, is there anything I may do for you? Mr. Winthrop's man may certainly ask."

Daniel had not expected this, and he studied the man's face for a clue. The expression didn't seem like that of the other fine men of Mr. Winthrop's acquaintance. John Pynchon did not seem to be talking down to him. He spoke like a man who understood the give-and-take of things—that was all.

"Well, since you asked—I would like to know what kind of wood that the cabinet is made from, over there."

Pynchon laughed. "A modest request, to be sure!"

"That, Daniel, is mahogany. It comes from far away—the Indies."

Oh yes, thought Daniel, the Indies . . . wherever they were. The English traded there—apparently for wood, too. Rum, he already knew about

—and of course Mr. Winthrop's black servant, Cabooder. From those Indies, too.

He stood there a moment, putting unfamiliar pieces together in his mind, when the other man coughed. He knew what that meant; he gave a quick but appreciative nod and went out.

As soon as their horses were no longer in sight of the house, William Deines spoke to Daniel. The day had only just turned warm, but Deines was already sweating hard, and as he spoke he mopped his brow with a cloth held tight in pudgy fingers.

"Mr. Pynchon prefers to call me William, as that is my Christian name, and I work for him," he said. "But as you work for Mr. Winthrop, and it is Mr. Winthrop that owns the mine, you may call me Will. It's how I call myself."

Daniel considered this logic and said, "Will's a good name."

"Robert showed you the warehouse this morning," said Deines. "You saw the corn, and the beaver furs, and the cloth and the other things—all of it? What did you think?"

Daniel wasn't quite sure what he thought. He was trying to figure it out, still thinking about the mahogany cabinet-wood from the Indies.

"I don't know. Where I come from, a man puts his land above everything else."

Deines gave him a puzzled look.

"What I mean is that he holds it—the land—more important . . . more important than anything that comes off of it." Daniel grunted. "Some of the gentry, you know, they don't do *anything* to get something off of it."

"Meaning that they get the likes of us to get it for them."

Daniel considered this.

"Well, yes, that's the way it is. But that's not what I meant. It's hard to say exactly, but it's like their *hearts* are in the land—the gentry's are. That's what important to them. So I don't know quite how I think about Mr. Pynchon's warehouse. It's certainly very large . . . with a great many things of many kinds in it."

Deines seemed satisfied with this accounting, and to sum things up he expressed a truth he'd heard many times.

"A man needs to make a living and provide for his family," he said.

"That's true enough," Daniel replied, but he didn't say the thought that was forming, "but how a man goes about can make a great difference."

For the rest of the afternoon they rode east, mainly in silence, each keeping to his own thoughts except to remark on some passing scene of appeal or interest. The trail was clear and well traveled, as it was the main route to Boston, and other travelers passed them going one way or the other. Deines seemed in no hurry. As evening approached he turned them off the main route at an Algonkian settlement that he told Daniel was called

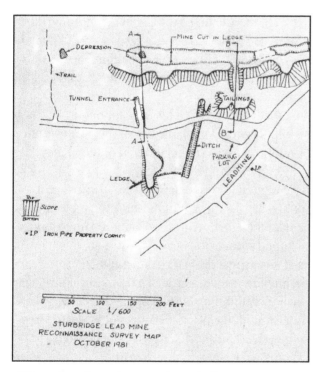

This section of a modern map shows the Tantiusques mine trench at the top, where Daniel and companions dug.

"Ashquoash—or some other heathen name." The trail south was not well marked, at places being little more than an Indian path through the woods, and they had to stop twice to be sure they were still on their route. As they were making their way over a hill, Deines called out, "that is the stream; I'm sure of it. It's not far now."

To the east they saw a large pond, its surface reflecting the pink of the setting sun. A plume of smoke drifted over the canopy of birch and oak trees. Riding closer to the smoke in the settling twilight, Daniel made out a large hut and then a second wood-frame building in a small clearing. A group of men stood around a fire, eating, and some called out when they saw William Deines.

By the end of his week there, working a black-lead mine confirmed in Daniel the simple opinion he had formed at the Hammersmith ironworks at Lynn and which his brief experience with the ironworks in New Haven had done nothing to alter. Everything about mining and the metal-making that came after was uncommonly hard and dirty work, and so the work tended to make the men who did it rather hard and dirty, too. Of the five other laborers at the mine, three of them he would be happy to never see again. But the other two he would be unhappy if he did not.

He had liked John Cockrill from the first. He didn't act angry and rough like most of the others. He was the first to awake in the morning, and though no one asked, he always had a small fire ready to share by the time the other men were awake and up. "Myself, I like a little something hot to start my day," he confided in Daniel. "It gets my own fires burning," and he laughed, a simple, open-hearted laugh.

He was happy to find that Daniel shared his taste for oatmeal porridge, and he shared his supply with Daniel, the two of them eating and joking while The Three Grumbly Ones, as Daniel thought of them, moped about the fire, scarcely eating and resisting the new day.

Well they might have wanted to resist, because the work, once it started after breakfast, kept up hard for the rest of the morning under the watchful eye and direction of Will Deines. The men clambered up to a ridge on the hillside and used picks and shovels to cut away at the soil, down into a vein of minerals. But the task was a great deal more difficult than just exposing the vein and shoveling out the black-lead. The vein was not regular or straight but seemed to meander, thinning here, dipping there, lost altogether at points. And once found, the black-lead was not loose and free but usually bound up tight in rocks. The men used heavy sledges to try to break the rocks, and many hours were spent in this slow toil.

They interrupted their work to take a noontime meal back at their camp, and then returned up the hillside to continue until early evening. Daniel joined as an equal in all the work, but apart from the companionship of labor, the men were slow to warm to him when they learned that he was Mr. Winthrop's servant. From occasional words and phrases he came to understand that the Three Grumbly Ones were all bound to others as well, which was no great surprise, since most young laborers were working off an indenture, as Daniel had learned long before. By exception, though, John Cockrill and his friend James appeared to be working only for themselves.

James Parker was less forthcoming with Daniel than John was, but Daniel found him on the whole an agreeable man, much raised in Daniel's estimation by having earned John's friendship. However, Daniel recognized that if John weren't present he might not have thought quite so well of James, as he lacked the industry of his friend and his unfailing good humor.

The week passed quickly enough. The summer weather was very warm, but where they worked in the woods the shade and occasional breeze brought some relief, and Daniel himself preferred to be active, anyway. Will Deines was sorry to see him leave, for he was a good worker and brought a kind of balance to the crew.

Will knew that Daniel would be stopping at the Pynchon house before returning to New Haven, he gave him a letter for Mr. Pynchon's warehouseman, John Mitchell, providing him a one pound credit for his labor.

With a heartfelt farewell to John Cockrill and their well-spoken hopes to see each other again, Daniel mounted his horse and made his way back as he had come.

When he arrived at the house overlooking the Connecticut River, Daniel was brought in to see Mr. Pynchon and gave him a brief report on the operations of the mine. The merchant received these in silence, punctuated only by a sober nodding of his head and pursing of his lips. However, when Daniel concluded, he again asked him what he might do for him before he continued his journey.

"I'd be pleased if you'd sell me some woolen fabric, so that I might have some winter clothing made for myself," said Daniel. "I have some credit from Mr. Deines and a few coins that I have saved."

"Very prudent of you," said Pynchon, "very prudent, indeed."

He directed Daniel to the small warehouse on the grounds, where Daniel made his selections of Kersey and Peniston woolens with John Mitchell, using the credit from Will Deines. Gathering up his yard-goods and a receipt from Mitchell, Daniel returned to the house for an accounting of the transaction.

John Pynchon wrote in his account book:

```
For Mr. Winthrops man Daniell Cone
3 y ¾ grey kersey at 7s 9d               OI   O   I
2 yds ½ Peniston                         OO  II   3
                                         02  OO  04

Recd by Joh Mitchell from Wm Deines      OI  OO  OO
& to be abated by you                    OO  07  08
                           rests         OO  12  08
```

"Very well, Daniel. This records our arrangement," said the young merchant. "As you see, the woolens cost 2 pounds, 4 pence. Your week's wages from Goodman Deines are noted. You have just paid me 7 shillings and 8 pence, which leaves you owing 12 shillings, 8."

He looked at Daniel levelly.

"I feel confident I can trust you for the remainder, Daniel–before the end of the year."

"And so you can," replied Daniel. "I will see that you receive my payment by way of Mr. Winthrop, or by other means."

Eliza, the servant woman, had been standing in the parlor, unnoticed by both men. "Begging your pardon, sir," she said in a voice a little too loud, "but Mr. Fellows just arrived and seems very eager to see you."

"Please show him in, Eliza. Stay for a moment, Daniel. Mr. Fellows is someone who would wish to know Mr. Winthrop."

A man some years older than Daniel and John, dressed in high leather boots and a loose red doublet, strode into the room.

"Excellent news, John!" he cried out, brushing past Daniel. "The Colony has granted me the 200 acres of land."

"I'm very pleased, Richard," said John, not at all surprised. "I'm confident that your inn will be a benefit to travelers."

"And so it will be. It will be good for them. And it will be good for me –and for you, God willing."

"Indeed, sir, God willing," John assented, apparently not having–or in any case, not wanting to show–too much eagerness for Fellows' enterprise. He turned to Daniel.

"Daniel, Mr. Fellows' undertaking may be of some interest to your master."

"His master?"

"Yes, the honorable John Winthrop, Jr."

Richard Fellows' indifference to man and servant changed completely.

"I would be obliged if you might mention to Mr. Winthrop this very favorable acquisition of property along the highway to Boston," Fellows proceeded, eyeing Daniel up and down, as if weighing the advantage of further effort.

Daniel noted the assessment and replied coolly, "'Favorable'? Sir?"

"Why, Goodman—?"

"Cone," said John.

"Goodman Cone, then—favorable' in that I may be in a position to assist with provisioning the lead mine – oh not, of course," he looked at John, "with the goods which Mr. Pynchon is already supplying, but with . . . other goods, and assistance," he added, vaguely.

"I see," said Daniel.

"Richard Fellows is the name," said he, "freeman of Hartford but now residing here. If you are not in too much of a hurry, I might write a few lines to Mr. Winthrop, if you would take my note."

Daniel said he would, and within five minutes Daniel had the note and was on his way back to New Haven, schooled a little more in the ways of merchant men.

A servant truly had little choice but to do his master's business. The only advantage to the servant, Daniel reflected, was what his business might be. And for all the seemingly constant moving-about of this year, the business of Mr. Winthrop gave him more opportunity than – well, it seemed more than any man he'd heard of. Certainly more even than Mr. Winthrop's servant Edmond, who the master trusted genuinely, enough to leave him in charge of his properties in New London when Daniel and the others moved to New Haven. Edmond had befriended Daniel when he joined Mr. Winthrop's service in 1656, and Daniel considered Edmond a good and true man. But now Mr. Winthrop was giving Daniel even more responsibility.

And so here he was again in Lynn, in the Bay Colony. His time in this little town along the Saugus River marked the passages on his journey in New England: prisoner of war, servant to Mr. Leader, who sent him to the ironworks; called away to Mr. Winthrop's service; and now back again on a master's business.

Daniel smiled to himself. It was good to be with his own countrymen again, as he had taken up temporary lodging at the place they called the Scotchmen's House. And it was very decent of them, these workers at the Hammersmith mine, to take him in. Still, with more than thirty of them and not enough beds, he was obliged to share his bed with another man!

But Hammersmith was not all a laughing matter; far from it. The men told him that during the past year the business of the ironworks had not done well. What exactly had gone wrong, Daniel could not tell, but the men feared that Hammersmith might close and they themselves be scattered and indentured elsewhere.

On this Monday morning, though, the din Daniel heard as he walked toward the ironworks was exactly as he remembered it, undiminished. True, as he came carrying his pack up the lane, his attention was drawn to the garden rows of Indian corn with their tall green stalks and tasseled ears sticking out. One young woman working there gave him a long look as he passed, but any sweeter thoughts he might have had were drowned out by the clatter of the millwheels and, a little farther off, the muffled roar of the blast furnace.

He passed by the blacksmith shop and the rolling and slitting mill, where he looked in to see the last stage of the processing. And there they were, all the wheels and moving platforms connected to the great waterwheels outside, meshing ingeniously to slit bars of iron into nails. He marveled at it anew; all this ingenuity and moving pieces of wood and iron, just to make nails! Daniel remembered what Mr. Leader told him, that this mill was so modern it was one of only a very few in the whole world. Be that as it may, the mill here was so different from the simple grain mills he had known in Scotland, it was hard to think of them as part of the same world.

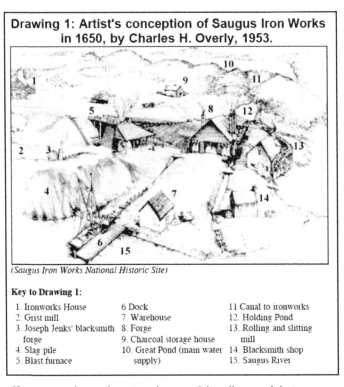

Drawing 1: Artist's conception of Saugus Iron Works in 1650, by Charles H. Overly, 1953.

(Saugus Iron Works National Historic Site)

Key to Drawing 1:

1. Ironworks House
2. Grist mill
3. Joseph Jenks' blacksmith forge
4. Slag pile
5. Blast furnace
6. Dock
7. Warehouse
8. Forge
9. Charcoal storage house
10. Great Pond (main water supply)
11. Canal to ironworks
12. Holding Pond
13. Rolling and slitting mill
14. Blacksmith shop
15. Saugus River

Hammersmith was the original name of the village and the iron works that later became known as Saugus.

He could have avoided it, but something caused Daniel to want to take just a quick look inside the forge, and so he crossed over the short bridge toward the clash and clang which grew ever louder. Outside the building he passed two of the four large waterwheels that spun in the creek, groaning and creaking and splashing continuously. This noise was nothing compared to the ungodly roar inside the forge. Just as he remembered it, the rhythmic shock of the giant hammer dropping repeatedly onto the huge anvil he could feel in his own body. He remembered once seeing four men—big, strong, burly men—struggle to move the hammer when the timber it rode on cracked; the hammer was that heavy: 500 pounds it was said. And its continuous lift and drop, lift and drop, lift and drop and the noise! It was enough to take over the rhythm of a man's own body.

On this summer day, the men he saw inside the forge, seven or eight of them, were stripped to the waist, sweating with the heat of three fires and blackened with their labor amidst charcoal and molten iron. The wind from the giant bellows fanned the forge flames, making the interior only hotter. Sparks flew off the anvils as the men pounded and reshaped and refined the reheated bars of iron that had been formed at the blast furnace. As he watched, the shouts of the men trying to be heard, the sparks flying, the red flashes leaping from the forges, and the constant slamming of the giant trip-hammer made Daniel remember what he had often thought when he would deliver charcoal to the forge. This was the Hell the ministers spoke of. This was the worst place he could imagine.

Continuing on his path he passed by the charcoal house, where he had spent many days, and hurried on to the manager's house with his pack, which had begun to feel heavy.

The manager could not see him, but his assistant, whom Daniel did not know, opened Daniel's pack.

"So, what is it?" the assistant asked, when he saw the heavy blackish lump.

Daniel wondered how much this assistant knew of rocks and minerals, and how much he should trust Mr. Winthrop's success to him.

"What does it look like to you?" Daniel countered.

The assistant just looked at him, noncommittal. Daniel did not like his eyes, which looked like those of a small, furtive animal.

"My master, Mr. Winthrop, was the first director of the ironworks," Daniel resumed. "He trusts that the abilities and knowledge of those in charge here have only grown in the years since his time. So he sent me here with this sample, which I took from his mine a day's journey from Springfield."

"Yes, I know all this from the manager," said his assistant, cooly.

Daniel was becoming impatient.

"And did the manager also tell you that Mr. Winthrop's letter asked for help—to know how this rock could *best* yield the *most* black-lead?"

"Yes," said the assistant. "We will assay it, and you will have our findings within a few days."

"Well!" said Daniel, "I'm sure this knowledge would be a great courtesy to Mr. Winthrop! And perhaps it will also prove a great benefit for others." And without another word, he turned on his heel and left the assistant, who eyed the black lump with an expression bordering on disgust.

Two minutes of hard walking later, passing the garden plot, Daniel paused, able to think again. He leaned against the fence and stared out over the food garden.

This insolent assistant would not have treated him this way if he had just been plain Daniel, another working man. It was because he was on an errand for Mr. Winthrop, whom the Scots all knew was one of the elect, one of those who held the power in New England, English son following father, like royalty, despite what they—the Puritans themselves—believed about the royals.

He didn't like it. He didn't like being judged because he was a particular man's servant or—he didn't like the word at all—"slave." He was five years into his servitude; most of it, he hoped, was over. He must exert more of his efforts to becoming his own man, to preparing for his own independent life. At 31 years old, he must look to marry and start a family. It could not happen until he was free, but he must prepare.

His eyes focused. The young woman across the garden was looking at him again.

Daniel looked back.

"A beautiful day!" he called out.

She walked toward Daniel, stopped, and replied in a modest voice, "That it is."

"That seems agreeable work you're doing," continued Daniel, feeling somehow encouraged on scant evidence.

"Oh, it is! I do like growing things," the maid replied and came just a little closer again.

"Tell me what you're growing, then, if you have a moment," he said, and when she offered a puzzled look he added, "—other than the corn, I mean. I can see that."

She laughed and seemed momentarily at a loss for a sensible rejoinder but walked a little closer still.

"I have just come up from New Haven where I've been so busy I've had little time for gardening," Daniel continued in a voice very nearly normal. "But I do enjoy helping things grow, myself."

"I know from your accent that you're a Scot," said she, "and I thought all Scots here were miners, sawyers, and the like."

"Well, I am a bit of all those things, now, but when I was younger I tended cattle on our farm. It was near Loch Lomond, my old home. "I miss it," he said, and speaking of it filled him with a little more emotion than he expected. What was he doing, he asked himself, in telling this girl these things about himself?

"From the way you say that," said the girl, "I'm sure that you do." And she left it there, neither encouraging nor discouraging him.

In the pause, Daniel focused on her soft, fresh cheeks and clear eyes and saw that she was a good deal younger than he, and that he probably should not detain her further.

"It's kind of you to speak with a stranger on this lovely day," he said. "But I'm keeping you from something you enjoy."

"Yes," she said, "but you know, men are just like plants. Under the right conditions the good Lord helps them flourish, too." And she smiled easily and began to walk away.

"Will you tell me your name?" Daniel called after her.

She turned. "Mehitable, daughter of Gerard Spencer."

"Thank you for coming to speak with me, Mehitable. My name is Daniel. Daniel Cone."

She gave a little curtsy and continued on into the garden. Daniel watched her move past the green, growing things, and he saw them, sprawling and upright, all seeking the sun.

For the next three mornings Daniel returned to the manager's office to learn what he could about the progress of the black-lead assay, and each morning he was disappointed that there was no news to be had. He was not completely disappointed in his mornings, however, as each day he passed the Hammersmith garden, and then he saw Mehitable Spencer again, for it happened that she was the manager of the garden, a position she said her father had arranged. Each day they spoke, and what they spoke about grew from the weather and the rewards of gardening and farming to topics a little more personal and a little less of the everyday world. Although Mehitable was younger than he, Daniel felt that what she lacked in years was made up by a well-grounded common sense and a cheerful disposition. He enjoyed speaking with her, very much.

On the third day she surprised him with an invitation.

"Well, Daniel," she said, "if I'm to manage the garden, I should continue working, but since I enjoy talking with you, and you say you miss gardening, why don't you come inside the fence and help us, so then we may talk when we are able?"

That seemed like a completely sensible proposition to Daniel, who, in truth, appeared to need very little persuasion. His time was his own while he must wait for the results of the assay, and so he spent a very pleasant day working close to Mehitable in the garden.

On Friday he felt the assay must be ready, and in this he was not mistaken. The unpleasant manager's assistant came right to the point.

"You can tell Mr. Winthrop we have done our best," he said. "We are not familiar with this black-lead material and the manner it harbors in rocks. At the mine, the men break the rocks with sledges to release the mineral?"

Daniel nodded.

"We did that, too"—and as Daniel was about to react, he added "—with half your sample."

"And what, pray you, did you do with the other half?"

The assistant sniffed, letting Daniel stew for a moment in his irritation.

"We heated it at the forge," he continued. "With a very hot fire, the parent-rock is much easier to crack open, yielding more of the mineral, we think, than by"—he looked for a suitably critical word—"*smashing* the rock.

"It's rather like cracking open a hard-boiled egg, if you see," the assistant concluded.

"Yes, I do see," said Daniel. "But will the mine need to have such a fire as here at Hammersmith, in order to obtain your results?"

The assistant looked at Daniel with an air of interest.

"That's a good question," he conceded, his manner unstiffening a little. "But I'm not sure we would know the answer, as we only had a limited amount of your sample."

He took on a more helpful tone. "I would say that you may just have to try with what fires you have available, and see what results you get. You may have to try several different ways until you find the best.

"I do have a few notes from the man who assayed the samples," he concluded, handing the papers to Daniel.

Reclaiming his rock, now broken in separate cloth sacks, Daniel said his thanks and departed, happy to be done with this hard man.

It was another matter completely when he passed by the garden. Mehitable came up to the fence when she saw that he was carrying his pack again. She waited for him to speak.

For a long moment he said nothing but searched her pleasant expression for a cue as to what he would say. Something that would keep that expression just so, to last in his memory, is what he decided.

"I have enjoyed meeting you, Mehitable, and seeing your gentle ways with growing things."

Was that a blush that colored her cheeks, Daniel wondered, fleetingly, or merely the summer light?

"I must return now," he continued, "first by way of the mine, to show what I have learned here, and then to New Haven and Mr. Winthrop. But I do hope that the good fortune that made us acquainted here, may someday occur again."

She smiled and met his gaze.

"And I do, too, Daniel. God speed."

Chapter 4. Judgment

I must say, John, that I shall be sorry to leave New Haven," said Elizabeth Winthrop, rising to leave their sitting room.

It had not been an easy conversation for either of them. John Winthrop disliked causing his wife any discomfort, and her great loyalty to him meant that she rarely expressed any views that would upset him or cause him to doubt his own judgment. She was sure that it would be an advantage to him to become the governor of the Connecticut Colony, as he had been elected. But she was not at all sure this new role and the re-settling in Hartford would be as much to her liking as New Haven. She had just begun to feel settled, and living near the seacoast agreed with her.

"I know. I am sorry that it discomforts you, Betty," her husband said, affectionately. "I believe it is my duty."

Elizabeth stood, considering this. The honeyed light of the fall afternoon flooded the room, warming a rectangle of floor in front of her and a crimson and gold wool rug, a favorite of hers that she had brought with them from England. She had laid it out in one colonial home after another.

John Winthrop stood and took his wife's hand. "Let us pray together," he said, and gently lowered Elizabeth to kneel with him on the rug.

"Oh Lord, hear our prayer. Give us the wisdom to do thy works and benefit thy people, and the humility to recognize that our knowledge is always imperfect and subject to your grace."

Elizabeth looked at her husband when he stopped and saw that his eyes were closed tight. After a long moment, she squeezed his hand and using his shoulder for support, rose. On her way to the door she turned and saw he had risen.

"I think you have done well to simplify your affairs with the mines," she said.

"True, I shall have another great claim on my attention. I am confident that Mr. Paine and Mr. Clark will market in an advantageous manner whatever black-lead is mined successfully."

"You did also engage them for your share of the ironworks here, as you said?"

"I offered to sell it to them," he replied, quietly, "but they would only lease it."

Elizabeth Winthrop weighed whether this financial disappointment warranted any further comment from her, but deciding against it, said only, "I shall continue the preparations for our move." With that, she left her husband to his own thoughts.

It had come as a good deal of a surprise, that letter in May from the leaders of the Connecticut Colony asking him to become their governor. His relations with the chief men of Hartford had been generally cordial, even though his father had differed sharply with their leader and town's founder, the Reverend Thomas Hooker. Hooker's dissatisfaction with the governance of the Massachusetts Bay Colony prompted his removal and that of his followers to found the Connecticut Colony in 1636. In 1638 Hooker and the elder Winthrop had exchanged lengthy and acrimonious letters regarding governance, in which Winthrop had argued that "it was unsafe and unwarrantable to refer matters of justice to the body of the people," provoking Hooker's retort that he would "chose neither to live—or to have his posterity live—under such a government."

But Hooker had been dead for ten years, and the younger Winthrop had maintained, separately from his father, close ties with the colony's leaders, including Edward Hopkins. In 1636, Hopkins was a prosperous London merchant, and he had managed and outfitted the expedition led by the young Winthrop that founded the Saybrook Colony. Starting in 1640, Hopkins had become governor of the Connecticut Colony, being re-elected to that role every two years through 1652. During Hopkins' era of leadership with the colony Winthrop had first been elected a magistrate, in 1651. He had been re-elected during the following years, but in the spring elections of 1657, inasmuch as he was living in New Haven, Winthrop did not participate. Regardless, the electors chose him as governor, invited him to Hartford in May, and invited him again in August. Now, as summer turned to fall, Winthrop realized that if he was to move to Hartford, he had best be about it before the snows of winter.

Betty would see to the organizing. Daniel could be relied on to carry out her instructions, and the negro Cabooder, with his great strength, would lead the other servants by example, lifting and carrying and moving all the household belongings.

The good men and women in their Sabbath attire, all in black, sat still. Mouths were shut—including the children's—and all eyes were fixed on the Reverend Davenport as he continued his sermon. The back of the church, where Daniel sat among the other servants, was the choicer place to be on this still, October noon, he reflected, as there the doors were allowed to be open to a hesitant breeze which made its way across the New Haven Green. The refreshing draft was a kind of justice, tempering the freezing wind that edged its way through those same doors in January, needling the servants with prolonged discomfort.

Mr. Davenport had raised his voice, suddenly making it easier to hear him at the back of the church, and his urgency pressed itself upon Daniel.

"It is in *vain*," the Reverend was calling out, his right hand raised toward the heavens, "for any sinful persons to expect God's turning to them in mercy and favor who do not turn unto Him with true repentance and reformation."

"True repentance!" Mr. Davenport exclaimed, and after a pause, dropping his voice into a hush of insistence, repeated "and reformation." He surveyed the rows of his parishioners, measuring the effect of these words.

A little sudden freshet of cool air wreathed itself around Daniel's brow, shaking him out of his thrall to the rhythms of the minister.

What about Cockrill and Parker? They were surely sinning against him, and he had had no sign of any repentance, no sign of any intent to make amends for the harm they were doing him.

"But!" Mr. Davenport began again. "*But* while they continue in their sins, they must *expect* that God will come forth against them."

The minister smiled a lofty smile and began again with renewed vigor and a louder voice.

"Indeed. He will come forth against them as the Lord of Hosts, commanding and ordering *all* his Creatures against them for their hurt."

Daniel strained to imagine that.

God. So much greater than any king, any commander, even Lord-General Cromwell—"commanding and ordering all creatures" to hurt the sinful.

Well, that'd be good. That'd teach them, it would. That's what they should expect, Cockrill and Parker—the rogues. The liars.

Daniel nodded his head back and forth, scarce listening to Reverend Davenport. Mr. Winthrop certainly was not the Lord of Hosts, but he was a fair man, a righteous man, and very influential. With what other master would he have had so good a care for any ailments ? Winthrop was the most respected doctor in New Haven . . . not that he needed much doctoring—not like that Mrs. Pynchon. But Mr. Winthrop was good to him, for he was a wealthy man who could provide good food, good clothing, and he did give him the opportunity to work for himself, to earn his freedom. True, being a man's servant meant he could be whipped for disobedience, though he could not see how that would ever happen to him. And he could be sold for a debt. Now that was another matter. That worried him. What had the minister said about God hurting the sinful? . . . Well, *he* wasn't sinful. Why should he be punished, if he loaned money to men who turned out to not be honest?

Brooding thus, dark thoughts crossed Daniel's mind.

Religious people were always so sure of their beliefs. But how well had the Scots been served by their beliefs? Queen Mary, the one they called Queen of Scots, what befell her? And the other Stuarts—Scottish royalty— hadn't Parliament promised not to harm King Charles when they took him prisoner? They beheaded him, too! Hadn't General Leslie been right at Dunbar, about waiting Cromwell out—but then the ministers told him how to wage war? A sorry mistake for thousands of Scots killed there! Hadn't the ministers told the young Charles that they would back him, for God was on the King's side and his people would rally to him at Worcester? Wrong again! Mistaken beliefs, all of them. And he somehow became entangled in them. They had brought him to be sitting in this church in an English colony.

Mr. Davenport was still speaking at the front of the church, something about the total depravity of men, all of whom were inclined to serve their own interests over those of their neighbor and to reject the rule of God. Daniel did not want to hear more. Sometime soon, he would have to tell Mr. Winthrop of the difficulties he was in.

The village of Hartford occupied a favorable setting beyond the meadows that fronted the Connecticut River. The two hundred residents had built themselves houses according to their means, but the abundant woodlands nearby meant that houses were built either of logs or, for those with the necessary equipment and time, trimmed boards. In the twenty years that elapsed since its founding, Hartford had taken on a more solid and substantial appearance, underscored by the bricks that were part of more recent houses. But of all the houses in Hartford, none was more solid and substantial than the home previously occupied by Governor Haynes, in which Governor Winthrop was now installed by the grateful colonists at their own expense.

Stables, barns, orchards, and gardens surrounded the main house. During the growing season the house would appear the pretty jewel in a crown of industrious husbandry and vigorous life. But on a cold January morning, a gray light cast a sickly shadow on the walls of a bedroom where lay the older two of John Winthrop's five girls.

Their father stood in the space between his daughters' beds, just as he had been standing since before the dawn, tending to them in their sickness.

"Oh, father . . . this fever! I shall be very happy when it is my turn for the cold bath," said Martha, lying in bed.

"I know, Martha," he replied, "and so you shall. It will be your turn very soon, I'm sure."

He smiled at her kindly, but he restrained himself from holding her hand or otherwise comforting her. She had the measles, and he knew that the skin sores, and the illness, could spread from the least contact. As a physician, a reader of books about medicine, and a close observer of those who were ill, Winthrop had developed an acumen about common illnesses which gave him confidence that he could be of use once a person was sick. But preventing an illness, and particularly a contagion like the measles – such knowledge was beyond him, and he chided himself that all of his girls had fallen ill with the measles despite his arts and science.

From the hallway appeared Molly, the servant girl, saying "We are bringing Betty back to the room now." That was the sign to leave so that his daughter could be returned to bed without any embarrassment.

Winthrop stepped through the doorway from the bedroom to see young Betty, supported around the waist by Molly, completely wrapped in towel and a thick robe. She was shivering but greeted her father with a bright smile.

"The bath does help so much!" Betty said. "My fever is gone, and I have relief again from the itching. Thank you, father."

"And I am grateful you feel better," he said. "Try to sleep if you can; you have had a restless night."

"You, too, father," said the young woman. "If you became ill, I don't know what we'd do."

He smiled at her concern as she passed him, and he withdrew down the hall toward the bath. He thought it unlikely he would be affected by the disease. He had suffered it as a younger man and been subjected to it again even before now, without contracting it. But he was not sure of its course. So prudence, as Betty counseled, was wise.

As he approached the room with the large metal tub in it, he heard the distinctive sound of snowballs falling into water. It did not surprise him.

"Good morning, Governor," said Daniel Cone, tending to the tub. "This was the way you wanted the snow?"

Winthrop had to laugh. The rounded snowballs that Daniel was dropping into the bath water reminded him of a peculiar cold soup.

"It does look odd, Daniel," he replied. "But I'm convinced this is the ideal way to reduce a high fever quickly. However, the water should not be so cold that it causes a severe shock, so you probably have enough snow in there now."

He tested the water with his hand and nodded his confirmation. Daniel placed the one snowball he held into a wooden trough.

"Now may not be the best time," Daniel said, drying his hands on the front of his leggings, "but may I speak with you about a personal matter, Mr. Winthrop?"

"What is it, Daniel? Is something the matter?"

"I had hoped not to trouble you about this, sir, but I'm afraid it can not be helped now." He sighed.

"Mr. Wyllys told me, when I brought him your message yesterday, that he had spoken with his sister before she left to return to Springfield."

"Yes? And what did Mrs. Pynchon say?"

"Well, sir, I am very unhappy to say that I am in some difficulty – oh, not with Mrs. Pynchon. She and Mr. Wyllys are trying to help me. It's that Mr. Fellows."

"Ah. Mr. Fellows." Winthrop knew the man slightly as one of the prominent residents of Hartford. But he had heard his reputation as a malcontent.

"Come, let's go into my study," said Winthrop. "I think Molly will be able to care for Betty and her bath quite well enough without us."

He led the way silently through the great hall of the house, where the governor traditionally hosted small gatherings. The walls of the hall were trimmed out in dark-stained wood, fine-grained vertical boards that rose to the ceiling. Five leather chairs sat in judgment over four smaller chairs and three stools, all of them empty – or at least such a fancy of judgment entered Daniel's mind as he crossed the imposing room.

Safe in the study, Daniel spoke again.

"Do you remember when I returned from Springfield last summer and brought that letter from Mr. Fellows?" he continued.

"Yes, something about an inn and his 'interest in being of service'—I think that was his phrase. Yes, I remember." Winthrop did not look particularly pleased with the recollection of the affair, for he had felt put upon.

"Well, sir, I would not mention him again, now, if it weren't that I feel he might press himself upon you, if you understand me – because of me."

Winthrop allowed himself a small smile and quietly sat back.

"Daniel, why don't you tell me exactly what has happened. This growing mystery is surely worse than the plain facts."

Winthrop listened seriously as Daniel recounted how John Cockrill had befriended him during his week at Tantiusques, and when he saw Cockrill again on his return to the mine on the way back from Hammersmith, Cockrill had asked him to stand with him in guaranteeing a loan to James Parker. Parker hoped to secure the loan from Richard Fellows. With the loan, Parker said he would have enough to pay for winter clothing for his older sister and her two young children in Boston, widowed that summer when her husband had died fishing at sea. Daniel agreed and joined Cockrill in guaranteeing the loan to Parker, which he in turn promised to repay to Fellows by the end of December. By then Parker expected to have earned more than enough from his work at Tantiusques. Or at least that's what he said.

"The difficulty is, your honor, that Cockrill and Parker left the mine not long after Parker received the loan, and no one—at least no one I know—has seen or heard anything of them since!"

Winthrop continued to sit quietly, reflecting no particular alarm, and spoke softly. "Can you tell me the amount of the loan, and your part?"

"Well, sir, John Cockrill and I agreed together to secure the loan of 15 pounds. My understanding with John was that we would each be responsible for half—if it came to that. But now that he's gone, and Parker, too, I suppose I'm responsible for all of it. That's what Mr. Fellows is saying, so Mr. Wyllys said."

Winthrop pursed his lips. Fifteen pounds was no small sum. For twice that much in personal property a man might be admitted to voting rights in the colony, assuming he was also first of a godly disposition. And fifteen pounds—if Daniel was obliged to pay Fellows—would almost certainly need to be advanced by Winthrop. This would also place Daniel further in his debt and lengthen his indenture: Not a desirable outcome.

Winthrop shook his head. "Fifteen pounds is a goodly amount."

Daniel's heart sank and he lowered his eyes.

"But to be honest with you, Daniel, I'm not so concerned about the money. I believe a resolution may be found about that."

Of a sudden, Daniel looked up.

"I am more concerned about your good judgment," Winthrop continued. "It can hardly be called a fault to be generous, which you were. But to be deceived. . . . You do see now how they deceived you?"

Daniel felt the back of his neck redden, and he knew he might anger.

"May I sit for a moment?" he asked.

"Of course. It's good to think about these things," said Winthrop.

Through the haze of his feelings, Daniel focused his memory on the moment of the loan agreement. He sat with an inward look and spoke again only after a long pause.

"Well, Mr. Winthrop, if I was completely honest with you, I would say something that might surprise you."

Winthrop laughed a little, in spite of himself.

"Please do."

"I have thought about this myself before now—gone over in my mind how I was fooled, it seems—and to be honest with you, I can not see the signs of their trick in the making. Was there a wink or a smile out of place, something perhaps a little too eager or too full of feeling about Parker's sister? Maybe she doesn't exist at all, for all that I know. But I am not so young or so untried in the world to miss such clues when they appear.

"It might make the situation easier to understand if I had missed them," he acknowledged, "but I don't believe they were there."

Winthrop pursed his lips and nodded his head with a look of assent.

"Indeed. Indeed," he said. "We do not in fact know that their intent *was* dishonest, to take the loan for other purposes and not repay it. We only know that they have not repaid it thus far."

"And that they have not been seen in person in some time," added Daniel.

Winthrop tilted his head and looked down his long nose at Daniel. "Well, I think perhaps we know what we can for now," he said.

"Thank you, Daniel, for bringing this matter to my attention. I will not be surprised if I hear from Mr. Fellows, and then we will need to make some arrangement with him and between ourselves. But in my judgment, you have done nothing wrong, and your reflection on this matter may in time bring you an advantage in understanding which you could not have gotten in any other way."

"I am honestly sorry to cause you any trouble, Mr. Winthrop," said Daniel, preparing to leave.

"I know that, Daniel. This matter reminds me that with the Lord, all things are known. With us and our imperfect knowledge, good judgment is hard work and always uncertain—if we are honest with ourselves."

The wooden clogs Daniel wore echoed across the rooms of the governor's house, gradually fading into silence, as Winthrop continued to sit at his desk, reflecting again on the distance between men and God.

With March and the loosening of winter's grip on Hartford came the summons to Daniel to train in the militia, a summons that came to every able-bodied man older than sixteen at some time during the year. The time for this annual service was not inconvenient to the governor, who in fact had exercised a little influence in its designation; the season of daily need for Daniel in the fields or about other business was still more than a month away. Daniel was therefore away from the governor's house one early March afternoon, training with the others, marching in file, kneeling in rows, firing their muskets at targets across a muddy field on the edge of town.

The governor was again in his study, as he had been for many afternoons during the winter, attending to affairs of the colony. He sat reading the notes of a recent session of the General Court, over which he had presided, and as he sat, he paused again to look across the room and consider what, if anything, he might be able to do about this controversy in the church.

Elizabeth Winthrop knocked on the study door and entered.

"Mr. Fellows would like to see you," she said.

"Very well. I have been rather expecting him," Winthrop replied.

He had only enough time to stack a few papers to the side of his desk when another knock on the door was followed by the rapid entry of Richard Fellows into the room, striding rapidly toward his desk.

"Your Honor, thank you for seeing me," he said, without any deferential tone to his voice.

"Mr. Fellows, you are just the man I was hoping to see," Winthrop responded, with disarming verve. "Do sit down."

Fellows, surprised by this greeting, quickly took the chair opposite.

"I have just been reading again the recent discussion in court over the controversy in the church. I am a relative newcomer to Hartford—and so I would value your opinion as a member of the church—and as one of Hartford's leading men," Winthrop continued, all smiles. "What are your views, if I may ask?"

"Well, sir, that is kind of you to ask, as I do have views, as you may know."

Winthrop offered an innocent smile and an inquisitive eyebrow.

"I shall tell you then," Fellows continued.

"Reverend Hooker—now he was a great man, I assure you. Too strict, some said—but to me, who heard him preach the word of God for ten years, he was a great man, and I shall tell you why. He had studied and learned, and he knew the truth!"

"More the virtue to him," Winthrop interjected, "to have gained such loyalty as yours."

"Well deserved, I assure you, well deserved. Mr. Stone, who took his place, can not replace him, if you understand me."

Fellows paused to study the governor's face for any sign of challenge, but finding none, pressed on.

"Now, sir, as to the controversy whether those who were baptized in our church but have not declared themselves of the Lord—whether they should have the same standing as committed church members—well, sir, I do not believe it is right."

Fellows leaned forward in his chair toward the governor.

"As you know, we are called to declare for the Lord after we have felt the spirit move in us—which is a wondrous thing; wondrous, sir!" Fellows took a pause, though his listener felt a doubt whether it was sincere or primarily for effect.

"But those who have *not* felt nor can speak of this spirit," Fellows resumed, "are *not* the same as we. I think the Reverend Stone *and* this so-called 'half-way covenant' with these people are far too liberal!"

Winthrop smiled.

"You are a man of forthright views, Mr. Fellows, and I appreciate that. Let me ask you, though, as was discussed last year and in our court, whether there is any virtue on the other side . . . that a sincere movement toward God, whether this should not be encouraged, as it may lead in time to a full commitment . . . and, in any case, that participation in the church will lead to a strengthening of our community?"

"I suppose what you say could be so," said Fellows, with apparent reluctance. "But it's not the sort of church or community that is best."

"That may be," Winthrop replied after a pause. "And still I hold out the idea that compromise may embrace a greater good."

He cleared his throat. "But you did not come to see me to answer *my* questions. Please tell me why you have come."

Fellows had removed his gloves and now put them, without ceremony, on Winthrop's desk. "It concerns your man, Daniel," he said. "He guaranteed a loan with another man, and now I expect him to meet his obligation."

"And why is that?"

"Because the man I loaned the money to, and his friend, Daniel's co-signer, have both fled the colony."

"And how do you know that?"

Fellows' eyes narrowed.

"Well, sir, it is my business to know men in several cities and towns. I have been told that the two fugitives, James Parker, the borrower, and John Cockrill, his accomplice, have been seen recently in New Netherland!"

Winthrop rose from his chair and walked a few steps to a bookcase where some of his scientific and medical books and instruments were held. Absent-mindedly he picked up a small magnifying glass and with it tapped his other hand.

"These are serious matters and a serious assertion," he said. "I suppose you would be willing to state your case in court?"

"Indeed I would," replied Fellows, without hesitation. "I am no stranger to court, and the truth is with me."

Again Winthrop cleared his throat. "Mr. Fellows, I believe you, and I think I can spare us the inconvenience and time of a legal action."

Fellows relaxed in his chair and sat back. "I should like to hear," he said, "pray tell me."

"I see two paths to recovering your money. For the first: As it happens, I have a long acquaintance with Governor Stuyvesant of New

Netherland, and although, to my knowledge, no such request has been made before between our governments, I think it proper to officially ask him to return the fugitives if he can apprehend them. That is, if he can not first induce them to repay the loan."

"This sounds like a path worth taking," said Fellows. "And what is the other?"

"I remember that you have inquired with me previously about offering your services in connection with the mine at Tantiusques. As the black-lead is mined there it needs to be transported to Boston for shipment to England or for other sale. If you are interested, we might contract to have you provide this carriage service."

A broad smile lightened Fellows' face. "A most interesting proposition," he said. "I am quite interested in it."

"Good," said Winthrop. "Then here is what I propose. Today I will compose letters to both Governor Stuyvesant and to the merchants Paine and Clark in Boston. If you return tomorrow and are satisfied with the letters, they will be sent; and we will ask for speedy replies.

"In the meanwhile, for your part, until these plans mature, you will take no further action on the matter of Daniel's collateral, nor shall you discuss our arrangements in public. Are you in agreement?"

Winthrop remained standing apart from his writing desk, tapping the magnifying glass in his hand, as Fellows considered the offer. It took him only a moment.

"I am in agreement, Mr. Winthrop—at least until tomorrow, when I shall return to review your correspondence, and if it be as you say, we shall continue in this wise."

Winthrop did not care at all for this doubt as to his word, and for a fleeting moment he wondered whether the compromise he offered the man was, in fact, giving him too many concessions, too much consideration. But this feeling passed into cool equanimity.

"Very well, then. Until tomorrow, Mr. Fellows. I may not be at home, but the letters will be available if you call after mid-day. And for now then, good day to you, sir."

"Good day." Fellows rose to approach Winthrop, perhaps to offer his hand, but Winthrop had moved toward his desk, and seated himself without another word, busying himself opening a drawer of the desk. He heard the door close before he looked up, then took a clean sheet of paper, upon which he wrote:

Much honored Sir,

Complaint being made to me by Daniel Cone that one James Parker (for whom he stands bound with John Cockrill for fifteen pounds due to Richard Fellows of Hartford) is with the said John Cockrill escaped to New Netherland, and understanding that they are there at present, upon this said complaint I thought it necessary to request this favour in his behalf, that you would please, upon examination of the case, to cause the said James Parker, and John, to be returned to New Haven by Joseph Alsop, or Mr. Lamerton, except they do pay the said debt or put in good security for the same the said debt, being now called for to be paid by the said Daniel. If there shall be the like occasion I shall not be wanting to

Governor John Winthrop, Jr.'s letter to Governor Peter Stuyvesant of New Netherland on behalf of Daniel Cone indicates the personal interest that Winthrop took in this private matter.

attend the furthering of equal Justice in any case wherein by any of yours the assistance may be required from Your affectionate friend and servant.

After signing his name, Winthrop dated the letter March 2 and turned over the sheet to adddress it to Peter Stuyvesant.

He was taking these measures to benefit Daniel, he thought, and only incidentally Fellows, so Winthrop paused as he considered what exactly he would say to his Boston mining agents. Daniel's review during the last year of the mine site and the opportunities and difficulties there had helped clarify for Winthrop what he might expect from this enterprise, and he had accordingly been acting to reduce his direct involvement and at the same time to secure any distinct advantage. A few weeks previous he had asked William Deines to confirm his title to the mine by seeking a confirmation of the deed from whatever local natives were then in a position of authority. Winthrop had only the day earlier received word from Deines that he had scheduled a meeting with the son of the Indian who had first signed the deed in 1644, and he had every hopes that the native would confirm Winthrop's ownership rights.

Winthrop picked up his quill again and composed a short note to Paine and Clark, asking them to give Fellows the opportunity to prove his ability to transport materials from the mine to Boston, and requesting a report of their discussion at their earliest convenience. He mentioned nothing about Daniel nor the specifics of his obligation, assuming that Fellows would be unlikely to raise these topics himself.

He had misgivings on this point of Fellows' discretion, but on balance Winthrop was inclined—absent strong evidence to the contrary—to hope in the latent goodness of his fellow man, rather than otherwise.

"Mr. Gardiner, come quickly, I fear for her life!" Praying, Lion Gardiner rose quickly from his knees and followed Arthur Howell out of his house. In the early morning light, Howell was running, and though Gardiner was three decades his senior he caught up with the younger man at the door to his house.

"What has happened?" Gardiner gasped.

A loud shriek from an inner room answered him. It was Elizabeth, Gardiner's daughter, sick abed a week with an unknown ailment. He rushed toward the room, past the hearth where Goodwife Simon sat nursing Elizabeth's baby.

"Mother! Mother!" Elizabeth cried out wildly.

Mary Gardiner squeezed her daughter's hand.

"I am here. I am here with you."

Her daughter's eyes opened, but their look was not outwards. "Double-tongued! Oh, double-tongued . . . Gar-lick!" she screamed and fell back, her body going limp.

The mother looked up at the men who had entered the room. "It has been thus for a quarter-hour, Lion," said Gardiner's wife. "We did not think to call you, at first. But it has become worse, and now she sounds more and more agitated."

Catching his breath, Gardiner nodded in understanding.

Arthur moved to the head of the bed and placed a cool wet cloth to his young wife's forehead. "Did you hear?" he said, his voice trembling. "She said the name of Goodwife Garlick again."

"This is her witchcraft!"

Shaking off the cloth and sitting bolt upright, Elizabeth shrieked, "A black thing . . . an ugly thing," and after a long moment, ". . . PINS!"

With this last word, the sick young woman collapsed onto the bed, shook once violently, and was still.

Mary Gardiner leaned over her daughter and, calming herself, felt the girl's breath on her cheek.

"She breathes—faintly," Mary Gardiner said, still holding her daughter's hand.

"Merciful God!" exclaimed Goodwife Simon, entering the bedroom with Elizabeth's baby.

They all sat: Arthur on the edge of the feather bed which he had so proudly assembled not many months before; Lion in a chair he plucked from the hallway; Goody Simon on a stool, holding and rocking the infant; Mary as before. No one spoke.

Hours passed.

Neither did Elizabeth Gardiner speak again, and that afternoon, with her parents, husband, and baby around her, the eighteen-year-old mother breathed her last.

The shock, the sorrow, and the uncertainty the survivors felt was submerged a little as all made the necessary preparations for her burial. At

that sorrowful event the next afternoon, a few of the righteous – a
forward – members of the tight-knit community of Easthampton tho
right to mix their heartfelt condolences to the bereaved father with an
attempt to explain the remarkable circumstances of his daughter's death.
Their explanation always included the word, "witchcraft." Lion Gardiner
thanked them for their condolences and nodded soberly.

Normally he was not the sort of man to be easily persuaded about
such a thing as sorcery. A soldier and military engineer by profession, his
habit of mind measured things visible, carefully and dispassionately. This
habit was ingrained from experience.

In his thirties he had been master of fortifications for the Puritans in
Holland, as they repelled the Papist Spaniards. This service called him to the
attention of certain Puritan lords who funded the development of a colony on
the Connecticut coast. Gardiner received the commission to build a fort at
the mouth of the Connecticut River, thereby fortifying the new colony of

*Lion Gardiner in the Pequot War, a watercolor painted by Charles Stanley Reinhart for the
Gardiner Estate, circa 1890.*

Saybrook, named after Lord Say and Sele and Lord Brook. John Winthrop,
Jr., younger than Gardiner and less tested in the world, was named the
governor of the colony. This was 1635. A year later, Gardiner had argued
strenuously with Winthrop against a plan to attack the local and bellicose
Pequot Indians for what Gardiner considered insufficient causes. When the

attack by laying siege to the Saybrook fort, three of
d, and one was captured and roasted alive. He
what the Pequots had done, but he was clearly
doned the attack on the Indians while he himself

quent brutal war against the Pequots, Gardiner
across the body of water that separated Saybrook and the
necticut colonies from a long island, ultimately helping to establish a
community there that became known as Easthampton. Puritans from Lynn in
the Bay Colony, seeking more land and fewer restraints, were among the first
settlers.

Distant from other English colonists, at the tip of an island exposed
to a hostile ocean, the residents of Easthampton, more than those of most
other places, turned to each other and knew about each other, for good and
bad.

Thus remote and with his preference for the measurable works of
man, Lion Gardiner was not inclined to believe things about his neighbors
without clear and compelling evidence. As in any place, Gardiner knew,
people might be reliable, hardworking, troublesome, peculiar, or many
other traits, sometimes one after another, or one alternating with another.
So he found it at first hard to believe that a person might be wholly possessed
by Satan and a witch, as his fellow townspeople believed Elizabeth Garlick to
be.

The Garlicks, husband and wife, were menial people, low and sullen,
ill-favored in appearance and befriended by few. The couple had worked for
him for a time, and he was not unhappy when they departed. But that the
woman could be possessed by Satan—well, if his own daughter had not said
so, and he had not heard it, Gardiner would never have seriously considered
it. But now his daughter was dead.

"Thank you, Daniel, for your errand."
Smiling at Samuel Wyllys, Daniel slipped off his clogs and placed
them near the kitchen fire, now burnt low, and put back on his soaking
boots, still slimy with mud from the unpaved earthen roads of Hartford, slick
from the spring rains. He stood at the kitchen door, ready to go back out

from the Wyllys home and continue his rounds delivering the governor's messages.

"I shall pray that all may be resolved fairly with Mr. Fellows," continued Samuel. "And do thank the Governor for providing this information for the court session. It will give me time to collect my thoughts."

"You're very welcome," said Daniel, hesitating to use Samuel's Christian name, which Samuel had offered once before. Daniel was several years older and of such a different set of experiences that Samuel, from his position of privilege, found him intriguing. If it were not that one was a governor's son and the other a governor's servant, they might have been friends; a lively current of good feelings passed between them.

"Well, I'm off on my rounds," finished Daniel, and was out the door.

Samuel's mother was in the garden, clearing out the winter's damage and preparing for a hopeful year. He watched as Daniel greeted her and she paused for a moment in her work, strongly framed beneath the spreading branch of an oak tree and its large trunk. The tree was just starting to leaf out; life was returning after a dismal, sickly winter. Inside the house was quiet. Samuel's wife, Ruth, was upstairs asleep, with the baby. There was no better time to consider Governor Winthrop's message, whatever it was. Samuel sought out his father's big armchair, and seating himself, broke the wax seal of the letter.

> Dear Mr. Wyllys,
>
> I would be indebted to you if you review our laws relating to witchcraft. We shall hear a troubling case, I believe, and for reasons that I shall explain to you, it were better that my own role in this matter be limited. I look to you to be alert and just. Enclosed a draft of the indictment. Yours, John Winthrop

On a second folded sheet, in another hand, Wyllys read,

> In the Particular Court, Connecticut Colony
> An Indictment: Elizabeth Garlick
> Thou art indicted by the name of Elizabeth Garlick the wife of Joshua Garlick of East Hampton, that not having the fear of God before thine eyes thou hast entertained Satan, the Great Enemy of God and Mankind, and by his help since the year 1650 hath done works above the course of nature to the loss of lives of several

persons (with several other sorceries), and in particular the wife of
Arthur Howell . . . for which, according to the laws of God and the
established law of this Commonwealth, thou deservest to die.

Samuel Wyllys sat back in the big chair and sighed deeply. This was
very hard, he thought, and for a moment he thought nothing else.

He had hoped there would be no more of these witchcraft
accusations. There had been none in several years. The last one in
Wethersfield, when the husband and wife were both hanged, weighed heavily
on his spirit. He had seen men and women newly dead since then; he had
seen his own father die. But the memory of these two, their swollen faces, the
terrible distorted expressions, struck him again with cold dread.

It was his father, as governor, who had established the law that made
witchcraft punishable by death. Governor Wyllys, in 1642, was only acting in
a way that was consistent with English law since the time of Queen Elizabeth,
and, more importantly, with the Bible. Samuel knew the statute, there were
few words and plain enough: "If any man or woman be a witch—that is, hath,
or consulteth with, a familiar spirit—they shall be put to death." The
problem, Samuel believed, was in establishing the proof. He did not like the
way people talked about witches; those who did were vulgar, impressionable,
and inclined to too much imagination. Where was the proof?

He fingered the watch in his pocket, taking it out and gazing at it, as
he always did, with pleasure. His father had left it to him, and in truth, he had
not seen a better one, a more handsomely made one. The hands of the watch
were delicately made and traced their way with precision and evenness.
Samuel liked that.

He became quiet again. Proof. He knew how they determined it,
with the women who were said to be familiar with Satan. They would look for
his mark in the woman's most private. . . .Well. Enough of that. Mr.
Winthrop had asked him to prepare himself. He must review the court
transcripts of the Wethersfield and Windsor cases, much as he would rather
not. Samuel knew where to find copies of them.

The sun shown warmly; robins sang in the trees along Hartford's
Main Street the morning of May 5. The day could not have been fairer as, one
by one, the Colony's magistrates entered the inn on Main Street. Usually

talkative, the innkeeper Jeremy Adams this morning was subdued, for though he did not know the business of the court, he had begun to guess, when first the wild-eyed woman was brought in with two guards, and another man with them, looking, Adams thought, like a sheep hounded by dogs. Then the gentlemen magistrates arrived, not together, as was their custom, but separately, as if not to call attention to their arrival. As they came in he greeted Mr. Welles, Mr. Webster, Mr. Talcott, and Mr. Wyllys, and pointed them to the room where Governor Winthrop's man had brought their wigs the previous evening. And he mopped his bald head, sweating from his earlier exertions.

Adams had taken pains to lay out the room as had been requested for meetings of the court, placing some stools at the back of the room, just inside from the street, the two tables at about the middle of the room, with chairs behind them, and chairs furnished in leather at the head of the room for the magistrates and Governor Winthrop. Adams had rolled out his best rug—the one with both bright and dark designs—between the tables and the row of chairs for the magistrates.

The room was filling, but Adams noticed that the governor and a gentleman he did not recognize remained standing outside the inn, talking very seriously—he could see that plainly—in hushed tones. They stood sideways to him, so that Adams could observe them both, and he watched them fall into silence, looking at each thoughtfully, for longer than men usually did, as if there was some old debt between them. As an innkeeper he considered himself an expert observer of manners and their meaning.

Adams turned away and went to speak to his serving girls, and when he returned to the great room, he saw that the governor had taken his place with the other magistrates, and that the unknown gentleman, now with a woman, had seated themselves in the audience.

The great room was nearly completely filled, despite the early hour and the very limited public announcement of the court session. The men of the jury had arrived, among them Matthew Allyn and Nathaniel Ward, who Adams considered friends. He must attend to the business of the inn, but he was very curious about what would come before the court, and he listened closely as Mr. Wyllys began the case, reading the indictment.

"Elizabeth Garlick, rise and face the court," said Wyllys. From behind, Adams could see that it was the wild-eyed woman who rose.

"Elizabeth Garlick, wife of Joshua Garlick of Easthampton, not having the fear of God before thine eyes, thou hast entertained Satan, the great enemy of God and mankind. . . ."

Ah, that's why! Adams said to himself. The reason he did not know some in his inn was that they had come from Easthampton, on Long Island, across the Sound, a place which had just fallen under the jurisdiction of the Connecticut Colony. The sheepish man was Joshua Garlick, and his wife was accused of being a witch.

For a moment, Adams stood stock still, rooted to the floor. A witchcraft trial! His first thought went to his young daughters, upstairs with their mother preparing for the day. They must not come through the great room; he must warn his wife. With a start he loosed himself from his spot and hurried to the back stairs.

When he returned the trial was in process. A man seated at one of the benches, apparently an official from Easthampton, read from a document.

"Goodwife Birdsell testified about the mysterious death of Goodwife Davis's child," the man read. "Goody Davis had told her that she had dressed her child in clean linen and Goody Garlick came in and said, 'How pretty the child doth look' and very soon after she added, 'The child is not well for it groans,'—those words exactly. And Goody Davis said her heart did rise and when she took the child from Goody Garlick, she saw death on the face of it."

The townsman stopped in his reading and lifted his head, drawing a long breath.

"And her child sickened presently," he continued reading, "and lay five days and five nights, and never opened the eyes, nor cried, 'til it died."

The great room was hushed. After a silence, Samuel Wyllys asked the Easthampton townsman to continue, and he began to read more depositions, but Jeremy Adams already had his mind made up. He left the room to tend his vat of beer, which was nearing the end of its fermentation and might require transfer to kegs.

Nearly an hour later, when he returned to the great room, wiping his hands on an apron around his waist, Adams saw that the trial had proceeded to examination of witnesses.

"Please be very clear about exactly what your daughter said to you then, Mrs. Gardiner," Samuel Wyllys was saying.

Adams could see from across the room that the young Wyllys's features were strained and his voice was dry. And so that's who *that* man is, Adam's thought; the one talking with the governor before must be Lion Gardiner – the hero of the war against the Pequots!

"I had been quite ill myself, so my senses were all very alert," Mary Gardiner answered Wyllys. "I remember quite clearly." She sounded sure, almost defiant, thought Adams. Likely not the best posture; and she is not English, he reckoned, listening to her voice. Perhaps she was Dutch, or French.

"When I entered the bedroom, Elizabeth looked very pale, and she told me—her exact words—'Mother, I am bewitched.'"

"'No, you are not well and not seeing clearly,' I said; 'You are asleep or dreaming.'

"'I am not asleep and I am *not* dreaming,' my poor daughter replied. 'I am bewitched.'"

"I wondered what then to ask," Mary continued, "and after some moments as my daughter stared into the room, I thought to ask her, 'Whom do you see?'"

"She said nothing for a long moment, but sat up in bed next to me, until suddenly, she shrieked, 'Goody Garlick! Goody Garlick! I see her at the far corner of the bed, and a black thing of hers at the other corner!'"

"These were her exact words?" magistrate Thomas Welles interrupted.

"Exactly," said Mary.

"And was Goody Garlick—the accused here—" Welles nodded in the direction of the wild-eyed woman, "was she indeed in the room?"

"She was certainly not," replied Mary, indignantly.

The great room fell very quiet.

"How had your daughter known Goodwife Garlick up until this time?" asked Samuel Wyllys.

"The Garlicks worked for my husband starting about eight years ago, when Elizabeth was about ten years old. Then and for a few years after, Elizabeth came into frequent contact with Goody Garlick."

"And how would you describe this contact?" asked Wyllys.

Mary Gardiner paused, searching for the right word.

"Cold," she said. "I would say that Goody Garlick was always cold to my daughter. Unfriendly. Once, not long ago, I remember Elizabeth saying that when she went to Garlick's house in search of her husband—Mr. Howell was about the neighborhood, and Elizabeth had sudden need of him as she was with child and not well—Elizabeth told me that Goody Garlick jeered at her when she inquired for him."

Jeremy Adams nodded his head slowly. There seemed a pattern in this to his way of thinking. It pointed to Goody Garlick's guilt, he thought. But now he wasn't completely sure. Spying an empty stool next to Daniel Cone, he sat himself down to hear the rest of this business.

And so it went, through the rest of the morning; witnesses, examinations, then instructions to the jury and a break for lunch—during which Adams became very busy indeed.

Early in the afternoon, the jury returned. It was over quickly, and the verdict rendered somewhat to Jeremy Adams' surprise. Not guilty.

Mrs. Gardiner slumped at the news and leaned her head on her husband's shoulder. The Garlicks turned to each other, at first looking only stunned, but then they embraced as their tears welled up. The onlookers began buzzing with their opinions. The bailiff stamped his staff hard on the wooden floor three times to restore order.

"Gentle and loving friends," Governor Winthrop spoke up. The room quieted.

"Gentle and loving friends of Easthampton," he continued, "although the jury has not found sufficient evidence to prove the charge of witchcraft, yet we well approve and commend the Christian care and prudence of those in authority with you, in searching into this case, according to the suspicions we have heard.

"We know that the majority of you voted to have this case brought to trial. This court now calls on all those of Easthampton to be neighborly and peaceable, one to the other, without just offense to Joshua Garlick and his wife. *They* should be the same unto *all* others. In security of this treatment, this court requires Elizabeth Garlick to appear before the court in Easthampton, at such time as that court deems appropriate."

Winthrop surveyed the Easthampton townsfolk present in the room, staying his glance for a long moment on the Gardiners. Satisfied that he had said all that he might in open court, the governor pronounced the court dismissed.

As those in the room began to gather themselves to go out, Adams turned to Daniel, still on the stool next to him.

"What did you think of the verdict?" he asked.

"I think it's a fair judgment, based on what I heard," replied Daniel. "I think it's better not to imagine things without proof; and better not to judge too quickly."

He saw that Adams appeared unconvinced.

"Well, as I see it, I suppose we shall never have perfect knowledge of ourselves and our own actions," he added, "let alone the actions of others."

Adams considered this. "That's very well said, Daniel."

And with that approval, Daniel joined the others making their way into the sunshine.

Chapter 5. Enduring Choices

The air of this September day, year of Our Lord 1658, hung dank and uncomfortable over Hartford as Daniel crossed the green in front of the church carrying a small hammer, some nails, and a few sheets of paper.

At the Colony's official posting board, Daniel put the papers on the ground and with the claw of his hammer began to pry the nails from the announcement of the week earlier, which read:

On Wednesday, the 8th of September, is appointed a Solemne Humiliation
in all the Plantations in this Collony, to implore the favor of God
towards his people,
in regard of the intemperate season, thin harvest, sore visitation by sickness
in several Plantations, and the sad prolonged differences
that yet remaine unreconciled in Church and Plantations.

Daniel shook his head, though whether about the proclamation, the weather, or something less definite, he could not himself have said. He had a feeling, and it just didn't quite feel right to him, this Hartford. It was more than the strange hot, then early cold weather, the disputes between members of the church, the trial of that Garlick woman; it was as if life here wasn't going anywhere that he could see. Thirty-two years old, no longer young, still not his own man, he was restless.

Daniel tapped the nails into the corners of the new proclamation without looking at it more, then bent over and picked the other papers up off the ground. Somewhere in the distance a dog barked, not loud but persistent.

❖

John Winthrop lay in bed, fussing. He very much disliked being ill, though he knew there was a cause, and that it was for him to accept. But what was the cause?

They were quite right to have declared the day of humiliation; it would certainly seem that the Lord was not happy with the people of Hartford. The weather had been wrong all year, looking back on it: too much rain, not enough sun, unsuccessful plantings, and now a poor harvest. The ministers of the Bay Colony were right, to a measure, in decrying the decline of virtuous behavior there—the lessening in church attendance, the wearing of showy clothing, the increasing lack of humility among the people. Three decades after the first of the Separatists arrived, New England— including this Connecticut Colony, founded by Hooker to be better than the Bay— seemed no longer as upright as it was, nor so clear in belief and purpose.

Winthrop inhaled deeply through the one nostril that was clear and breathed out slowly through his mouth. In truth, he, too, was not quite right with himself. Perhaps that was why he was not feeling well.

He was 53 years old. Although he generally felt well enough, he felt himself . . . well, he didn't quite know how to express it. Much that he would have thought to have accomplished had failed to resolve itself favorably, despite his devotion of energy. A dispute among those in New London, including many of his old friends and associates, had led to a bid of some to secede from alliance with Connecticut and become part of Massachusetts. Winthrop, as a commissioner of the United Colonies, had presented his argument in favor of Connecticut. But he worried he might not prevail.

His son, Fitz, was in England, and Winthrop was not confident yet in the young man's ability to thread his way through the oft-entangled social and political fabric of London. Winthrop wrote him just the week earlier, when first abed: "Be careful to avoid all evill and vaine company," he had written, specifically cautioning Fitz against such excesses as wine and other strong drink, which he felt never agreed with members of the family.

But now, as he continued himself ill in bed, Winthrop reflected on what was dissipating his own energy. "Too many enterprises," Betty had said, simply, when he had asked her that very question recently. There was truth in that, hard as it was for him to accept. If there were too many, how should he decide which ones to give up? He inhaled sharply again and kicked at the extra blanket covering his feet.

He remembered what his father had said to him when he was a boy. "Leadership, my son," he had said, "is most certainly a calling from God, and woe to that man who has been called and does not obey."

Winthrop lay there quietly for a long moment, propped up on pillows. Then, with a start, he threw off the covers and walked quickly across the bedroom to where a small stack of papers lay. He brought them back to bed, and leafing quickly through them, pulled out one dated March 29, addressed to "the Most Worshipfull Mr. John Winthrop, Governor of Connecticut." In it he spotted,

> For the cariage of the lead to the waterside Richard Fellows is vary willing to engage, first by going a turn or two upon trial, and after to go upon a more certain price. . . .

The letter was signed by William Paine and Thomas Clark.

He put the paper down. The Boston merchants would know how to manage the headstrong Mr. Fellows and prosecute the venture. No impediment there. As for himself, he must further reduce his involvement with this grubbing in the earth.

He snatched clean sheets of paper off the top of the stack, again took himself out of bed, wrapped himself in his robe, and took up his writing quill at the small desk in the room's corner.

He wrote to Paine and Clark, offering to lease the mines at Tantiusques to them for a period of years, to be operated by them as they saw fit, while he would receive the value of only a third of whatever their profits.

He folded and sealed that sheet, and a doubt crossed his mind. Quickly he took another clean sheet and began a note to Fitz. After taking a few words to introduce the topic of the leadmine, he wrote all in a rush,

> "There is some black-lead digged, but not so much as they expected it being very difficult to get out of the rocks, wch they are forced to break with fires, the rocks being very hard and not to be entered farther than the fire maketh way, so as ye charge hath been so greate in digging of it that I am like to have no profit by yesame."

Some more lines, and he was finished. He sat there quietly. No trumpets had sounded, no clear voice had come to him from heaven. But he had made a decision and now saw a clearer path ahead where before a thicket had lain.

John Winthrop took himself back to bed, and as he dropped his robe and placed himself under the blanket, he felt much more comfortable.

The Saugus River shone like a ribbon in the May sunshine out past the edge of the field. Hannah Spencer and her grown children, John and Mehitable, were preparing the soil for spring planting, while Hannah's youngest, Nathaniel, slept peacefully in a basket on the ground in close sight of his mother. Looking up from hoeing clods of still-damp earth, Hannah could see her husband walking from the house toward them. Gerard was still small in the distance.

She noted his urgency and saw him mop his bald head, warmed by sun and his exertion, as he approached. He was smiling as he arrived.

"Hannah, I have made up my mind," he said, without preamble.

Hannah put down her hoe. A few feet away in the row, John and Mehitable paused.

"We shall move to Hartford—this fall, I think."

"Well, indeed!" Hannah replied. "What is your thinking?"

"Come. Walk with me," he said, and taking his wife by the arm led her away from her work and the children.

"Look after Nathaniel, Mehitable!" the mother called back.

Gerard tucked his wife's arm more closely to his side and patted the back of her hand, as he resumed.

"I know it will cause us much labor and will in particular not be easy on you," he began, his voice softer. "I just believe this is best for us, and in particular for the children."

"You're awfully full of 'particulars' this morning," his wife said, a jest in her voice, "so I suppose I should hear them all."

So he reminded her of the letter he had received the week before from his brother, Thomas, in Hartford, telling him the news of the disruption in the church. Thirty of the leading men of Hartford had decided to leave the town and found a community more to their liking elsewhere.

"With all these families intending to leave Hartford, there will be opportunities to purchase their lands, Thomas says," said Gerard.

"Yes, this seems very likely," Hannah agreed.

"I might be able to provide land for our children in a way that I could not here in Lynn—close to us and on favorable terms," her husband continued. "The removal of the others from Hartford is much like the removal from Cambridge and Lynn which gave us our first opportunity here."

"And it would do my heart good to live again near my brother, after all these years."

Hannah studied her husband's face and saw the kindliness in his eyes, the care for family. It endeared him to her, despite the difficulties they had shared – and those that she alone had borne, as she bore a new child for him every other year since she was eighteen years old. Now she was forty; there were eleven children, and John and Mehitable, both in their twenties, must leave the family before long and make their way in the world. All this passed through her mind while she thought of what must be done next to move her family to a new home in a short time.

She removed her arm from its link with her husband's and turned to face him. She heard the river rushing nearby.

"Hartford may be better for the family, but we can't possibly leave until the fall, Gerard," she said. "We've just begun to plant. We'll need the harvest. All the arrangements will take time."

Gerard looked at her, this small woman in a black bonnet with a crease of soil across her forehead and clarity in her eyes, and his heart softened more.

"I agree. Let us be together in thought and deed . . . truly together, Hannah."

They turned together back toward the row where Hannah had been working.

"I am very fond of Thomas," she said. "He is a good man, and his furniture-making earns him a good living."

" –and admiration and respect, I should say," Gerard added. "The good will that people have toward him will ease our way, Hannah. Think of that. We shall not be starting over."

John and Mehitable stopped their digging and hoeing again when their parents approached.

"You will tell us about Hartford, won't you, father?" the young woman asked, giving him her fairest smile

"Of course," Gerard said.

"I see a great opportunity ahead for our family, and most of all, I hope for you."

Edward Whalley saw it all again:
A bitter cold January morning, the king wearing his cloak, standing before the scaffolding draped in black. The open square in front of Whitehall

full of people, between them and the king the regiments on foot and horse. The occasional word making its way through the biting air to Whalley, astride his horse in the throng of the others with Cromwell. King Charles speaking, standing next to his Bishop, an expression of resolve and composure on his face.

> *A sudden moment of complete stillness; the king saying clearly:*
>> *". . . Sirs, it was for this that now I am come here. If I would have given way to an arbitrary way, to have all laws changed according to the power of the sword, I needed not to have come here; and therefore I tell you—and I pray God that it be not laid to your charge . . ."*
> *The king looks about the circle of rebels arrayed in front of him.*
>> *". . . I tell you, that I am the martyr of the people."*

Whalley's leg wound throbbed. He saw the parchment again: the warrant of execution.

His hand picks up the quill, dips it in the black ink, and signs, right below his cousin Oliver.

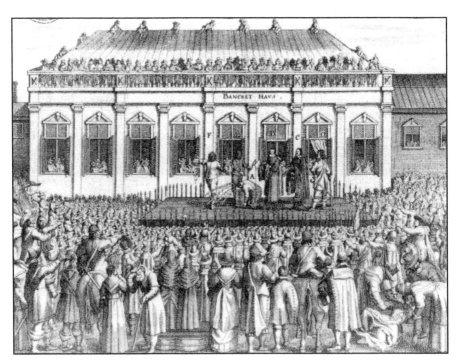

The beheading of King Charles 1 is depicted in a contemporary illustration.

The king mounts the scaffold and speaks again in a louder voice. "I go from a corruptible to an incorruptible crown, where no disturbance can be —no disturbance in the world."

The king bends down. Whitehall is hushed; no one breathes. The glint of the axe slices the morning air – and the executioner holds aloft the severed head. The crowd gasps and contracts. Whalley's horse shakes, and the cold sinks deeper into him.

And now, eleven years later—1660—after all that blood and strife—blood and strife and zeal to create and support the Commonwealth—the King's son is restored to the throne. The order given for capture and trial of the regicides.

Certain execution would follow, but not a swift death; the regicides would be treated as the worst of treasonous murderers, fit to be made an example of. Drawn and quartered. Disemboweled. God in his mercy might let them die first, but Whalley himself had witnessed such treatment, and the horror could be prolonged, as he well knew. Immediate flight, leaving wife and family behind, was his only course.

God would remove this new king, in time, he believed. God would decide. And then he would return to a freshly cleansed England.

The harbor at Boston was in plain view in the mid-summer sunshine. All that remained was to dock and seek out Governor Endecott. That would be first. Perhaps they would remain here in the Massachusetts Bay, safe from the agents of Charles II in this Puritan stronghold. Perhaps they would go to New Haven; the devout Reverend Davenport would harbor them.

God would decide.

Whalley turned on the deck to look for his companion, his son-in-law, William Goffe, who readied their meager belongings for disembarking. Fugitives, at their age, alone in the world; both in their fifties . . . an age when they might have hoped to enjoy the rewards of virtue and the pleasures of family. What struggles they had endured together! . . . At Dunbar, that terrible day, Whalley had had two horses shot from under him, leading the charge; Goffe had commanded a regiment, inspiring them through desperate hours. And then the Lord God had delivered them a great victory!

Surely in His justice and mercy, He might do so again.

The family certainly had quite a few children, Daniel mused. What had he heard: a dozen? Isn't that what Thomas had said?

In the early morning light, Daniel finished dressing, thinking ahead to the work of the day. He decided that the likelihood of getting his clothes dirty argued against wearing his buckskin breeches, which were harder to clean than cloth. Instead he pulled on his linen breeches, then his long stockings, the canvas boot hose over them, and finally his leather boots. He tucked his shirt into his breeches but planned to just carry his doublet; unless a cool wind came up, he wouldn't need it.

He tied his long hair back with a leather thong, and grabbing his two-handed saw, he left his room.

Thomas Spencer and his son Jared were waiting for him at their cottage, where after collecting up some more woodworking tools, the three of them began the long walk out of town to the home site.

"I'm glad you're helping today, Daniel. The building will go much faster with your skills."

"Well, I'm happy to help family of yours," said Daniel. "What sort of building are we going to work on?"

"A proper framed one, you'll see," replied Thomas, "—nothing like the kind that I made when I first arrived here myself in 1637."

Jared's eye caught Daniel's with a friendly warning of a long story to come, but Thomas intercepted the glance.

"To make a long story short, then," he said, "the first houses—mine included—were little more than cellars shoveled out of the earth, a few boards hastily erected and some thatch over the top for a roof. Quick enough for you, Jared?"

The father laughed, then the son and friend.

"But it was just as well we were simple and quick about it, because that was the year of the war with the Pequots."

Daniel said nothing, knowing already more than he wanted to, about war. But Jared was still young and untried in battle, and his father's exploits against the natives made a story he did not tire of.

"Tell him, father, but especially about what you did."

Thomas Spencer drew himself up and stopped. "Daniel may not care for such tales, and to be truthful, there are parts of what happened that I do not care for, either. Not at all."

"A man does things that he must, even when they cause him grief after," Daniel offered. "Sometimes he does not know enough before . . . to avoid the grief—"

"True," said Thomas.

"—and so I think that what a man finally learns from battles and other struggles can help him, if he think of it as honestly as he can," concluded Daniel.

This was wisdom, Thomas thought, and though he had not expected to hear it from Daniel Cone while walking on the road, he respected it and thought afresh of what his son might hear from him. He sat down along the roadside on a patch of short grass, and the younger men followed.

"It has sore bothered me, these last twenty years, what we did," Thomas continued.

The father saw his son's look of quiet alarm and responded in earnest.

"Oh, the Pequots murdered two—or four—of our English, as we were told. I do not know for certain. And they were a warlike, hostile group of heathens such as I have never seen before nor since. They certainly deserved some measure of rebuke, for if we had shown ourselves weak or less, that would have only emboldened them more and been the worse for us."

"So what is it that has troubled you, then, Thomas?" asked Daniel.

"I spoke of measure. I don't know; it is perhaps more with me than with other men. What I do, making furniture, requires a very pretty sense of measure, you might say, since if two legs are of different measure, the chair won't be right, of course. But more than that, I often think that inside the idea of measure—sort of the soul of it, as you might say—is proportion . . . how large the back should be, compared to the seat and the legs . . . and also to the seat and the legs of the man the chair is for.

"It seems to me that a proper measure is a sign of God's favor, or so I have often thought," Thomas said, and paused. He laughed softly, as if at himself.

"I see what you mean," Daniel said. "It's not something I've talked of this way before, but it speaks to how I feel when I see a man—or a woman—whose elements all seem to be fair with each other, all in proper measure and size and shape."

Jared looked at Daniel with a new kind of appreciation for the older fellow, an ability to put things in words that he felt but could not quite express.

The younger men waited while Thomas handed around sections of an apple he had taken from his pocket and quickly cut with a knife.

"Yes, Daniel," he said, "you understand what I mean. And so this is what has bothered me from long ago."

Daniel stopped from chewing, waiting for the rest of Thomas's thought. All three were quiet for a moment.

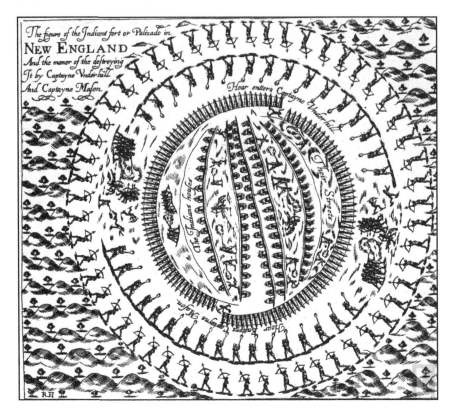

This highly stylized reconstruction of the attack on the Pequot fort is from combatant Capt. John Underhill's News from America *(1638). The colonists shoot at the palisade (inner ring) while their Indian allies back them up by firing arrows. What actually happened continues to be disputed.*

"We English gathered to attack the Pequots in their village, to correct the wrongs they had done us. There were two villages near Mystic, one with their braves, and another with men, women, and children. It was this one we came to, in the middle of the night."

He sighed. "We were like men in the dark, not really understanding what we were about."

In the early morning light, Thomas Spencer looked ashen, in remembering.

"There were about 80 of us. Their village was surrounded by a palisade of logs. By the light of dawn we circled the village and on command fired all at once into the holes in their palisade. That awakened the braves who were inside the village, who came out to defend their wives and parents and children.

"For me, what happened then is still like a bad dream," Thomas continued, after a pause. "Broken, jagged pictures . . . the cries of children in terror . . . my hand holding a sword . . . then suddenly wildfire rushing at me, filling everything. Our commander had ordered fire set to their wigwams. I didn't do it. . . .

"No, don't think of me as more virtuous; it had already been done. We killed many Pequots—men, women, and children. Many."

None of the three spoke for a long moment.

"In years after, the colony made me a sergeant of the militia, but I never wanted it. And, God be praised, I have never been in a battle since."

Daniel stared at Thomas. He stared but was not seeing him, instead saw the fragments of battle that he, too, had seen—fragments of the story of his life.

"I am sorry for you, Thomas," he said, quietly, focusing now on the other's face. Their eyes met, and a sad knowledge passed between them.

Slowly, Thomas rose, and the three resumed their way, in quiet for some time.

"Tell me about your brother, then, and his family," said Daniel, breaking the silence. "Where are they from?"

Thomas passed a few minutes telling Daniel a little about his younger brother, about how the five brothers had all come together from England in 1634; how they were descended, he believed, from a Spencer who had been a signer of the Magna Carta—a bit of English history he tried to explain to Daniel—and how Gerard had married and stayed in Lynn, became an ensign in the militia, operated the ferry across the Saugus River many years before; and over the years was "associated," Thomas said, with the Ironworks.

"Oh, really, how so?"

"Well, there were different capacities over the years, I think. And his oldest children worked there, as well, I believe."

"You know that I worked there for a time, don't you?" asked Daniel.

"Really? Well then, perhaps you'll recognize them."

"I don't know," said Daniel. "Perhaps. What are the names of his oldest children?"

"John—a stalwart young man. Strong. And just as fair and clever as he is strong is the second oldest, Mehitable. As 'bonny a lass' as you could want—as you Scots say."

Thomas smiled broadly. Jared nodded in agreement.

With a shock Daniel remembered that that was the name of the girl at the Ironworks farm.

No, it couldn't be the same girl. And yet he quickened his pace.

"There it is!" Thomas called out as they came to the top of a rise. Ahead before them was a large field, perhaps several acres across, with a home site in the center of the acreage, with what appeared to be at least a large garden on the near side of the cottage. Some people were standing and moving outside the cottage.

"This was a wise purchase," said Thomas. "The house isn't large enough for a family of their size. But it's built soundly enough on a good timber frame."

Daniel could see as they approached that the two visible walls of the structure were finished with wooden clapboard, and the fireplace chimney appeared to be made of bricks. These were good signs. It seemed to him that the roof was thatched on one side and shingled on the other. He clucked his tongue.

"So what is it your brother wants to make?"

"He wants a separate building, about 20-by-20, adjoining the one you see. He's had most of the timber cut and the post-holes dug, so he thinks we can make good progress right away."

That could be, Daniel thought. But this would not be a project for a single day, no matter how hard they worked.

Jared waved to a couple of the family members who had noticed the three of them approaching, and as they drew nearer, one of these came down the path to meet them.

"Mehitable!" Daniel exclaimed, under his breath, when he could see her clearly.

"So you have seen her before," Thomas said.

"Oh yes! Yes, indeed."

"Who *are* they?" Molly, the serving girl, asked Daniel, as he walked toward the door to go back to the stables. "I've never seen men in such . . .

finery!" She giggled, recalling the ruffled shirts, the handsome tall boots, and the scent of fresh spice that seemed to exude from the two young men as moments before they passed through the governor's great room, escorted by the governor himself.

Daniel turned back to her.

"Hush, lass. They're from the king.

"King?" What king?"

"You're toying with me, now. Sure you've heard? Charles Stuart is King Charles II of England. And Scotland. He's a Scot, you know."

"Yes, I know." And she also knew that Daniel was a Scot, and the way she spoke the phrase she meant to convey—something, she daren't say what—to Daniel.

But he was remembering the last time he spoke the name of this Charles as king. A great clamor and shouting, the rearing of a horse, smoke, a sword blade . . . pain.

"Daniel?"

Daniel surfaced from his reverie.

"What?"

"How do you know they're from the king?"

"They told me, lass." And seeing that such a short reply pricked the girl, he added, softer and confidential, "They seemed quite proud of it."

She continued to look at him.

"Well, so . . . do you need some help, Molly? Something I can do?"

It was her turn to start. She looked up at him through long eyelashes.

"Oh! Well, thank ye, Daniel. You could bring in a load of wood for the kitchen fire."

By the time Daniel returned, the girl was herself returning to the kitchen from the interior of the house, and her face was flushed with her errand.

"Daniel," she exclaimed, "Mr. Winthrop wishes to see you. Now. In his study."

At the study door, Daniel's knock was greeted by Winthrop's most courteous voice.

Inside, the governor was all smiles.

"Daniel, these gentlemen, Mr. Kellond and Mr. Kirke, are upon the King's business, and tomorrow I want you to prepare my horse for an early departure so I may start with them on the next stage of their journey. And now I'd ask you to see them properly settled for the night. They have had a strenuous ride, with more to come, I warrant."

"Certainly," said Daniel.

Mr. Kellond and Mr. Kirke, with suitable smiles and appropriate tones, took their leave of the governor.

As he was leaving the room, Daniel was addressed again by his master. "And Daniel, when you have finished with the gentlemen, please return to me."

Daniel nodded his understanding, brought the young men to Molly, who, after a moment's fluster, led them pertly up the stairs toward the guest room of the governor's house. Daniel returned, as bidden, to the governor.

"Sit down, please," said John Winthrop, his tone no longer honeyed, his manner more familiar, as it had long before become with his preferred servant.

"The arrival of these two men has great meaning for us," he continued, seated across from Daniel. "I can not speak about their errand for the king. But it makes me more concerned that young King Charles is alert to enemies of the Crown. And this is not good for our colony, not at all."

"Now, I think you know that I have been charged to go to England, on the colony's behalf. You do know this, am I right?"

Daniel nodded.

"I believe I must leave this summer, Daniel, as I feel some urgency in this business. And this will have a consequence for you."

Daniel drew a sharp breath. He had no desire to go to England, if that's what his master asked. He looked down.

"Nay, don't be alarmed," Winthrop continued. Daniel saw that he was smiling. "My necessary departure means a great change for you as well."

Daniel's heart lept up in anticipation.

"Before I go, I will release you from your service to me."

These words pushed Daniel back in his chair, speechless with surprise and sudden hope.

He sat there for a long moment, silent. Winthrop sat across from him, watching thoughtfully.

"I shall be very grateful, Mr. Winthrop," he said, at last. "Very."

"Then that is good. We shall speak more of it in time."

Winthrop arose from his chair, signaling their conversation was over for the moment. The governor walked quickly to his bookcase, as if looking for something particular there. His mind was becoming full of the challenge ahead, the necessity of obtaining the royal charter for Connecticut, the inevitable snares and pits along the way. If he would succeed, how much a service to his people . . . how much a proof of himself.

He reached for a leather binder that contained his father's letters to him and held it in his hands, not opening it at first.

After a moment, Daniel let himself out of the governor's study, then out of the house.

In the late spring night, Daniel stood and looked up at the wide and starry sky, and he breathed, long and deep, as if he had not truly breathed for years.

Daniel came out of the church in a hurry, not wanting to lose sight of Ensign Spencer. There he was. His bald head gave him away as he removed his hat. Daniel hurried up on the older man's outside shoulder, so that his request would not be heard by all his family.

"Might I have an opportunity to discuss an important matter?" he asked Gerard Spencer.

"Why Daniel!" the latter exclaimed. With a look at his wife, Gerard replied, "certainly." The Spencer family continued alone as the two men walked along quickly together.

By the time they had arrived at the Spencer home that Sunday morning, Daniel had said all that he had planned so carefully to say to Mehitable's father, punctuating his remarks by stopping in the street at points of emphasis. He was emphatic about his great desire to marry Mehitable, but as they crossed the threshold into the Spencer's front room, Gerard Spencer—despite smiles and nods—had yet to respond in any definite way.

"You know me to be a plain-speaking man, Daniel," he now began.

"I do, and that is one reason I find it a comfort to speak with you. To be honest, sometimes the men I meet through Mr. Winthrop are not so plain, and confusion breeds more confusion, I think."

"Very well said, and quite to the point." He leaned his walking stick against the wall, took a seat, and motioned Daniel to a chair opposite him.

"As I was saying, I'm a man who says what I think, and I ask what I must. Well, Daniel, I have had the opportunity to view you from close over these last months, and I have seen nothing, even thus close, that a jealous father could find fault in."

He paused. "I can see by your smile that you are questioning something."

"'Jealous' did not seem a word that suits you," said Daniel.

Gerard laughed.

"Yes, about most matters I am not the jealous sort, not envious—not 'covetous,' as Reverend Stone said this morning. I am not jealous of the man my daughter will marry; like any other father I should be happy to see her married well. But while she still is mine, I am jealous of her future, Daniel, and so I should like to be satisfied on one question that will shape her future and to which you have the answer."

"Only ask and I shall tell you," replied Daniel, immediately.

"Very good, I shall do so, but will you swear your truth by the Bible?"

"If that is your wish."

Mr. Spencer left the room and returned in a moment with his treasured copy of the Geneva Bible and put it on the table in front of Daniel. His face had become solemn and strained, and when he spoke his voice was low and quiet.

"I shall ask you the question that is my purpose, but this question is of such a personal nature that it is only right that I tell you why I ask it." It was his turn to sit back, and after clearing his throat he resumed.

"As you know, I came to the colonies when I was still not twenty years old, but before coming here I had seen and spent a little time in the city of London. What a place it was for a young man from the country! . . . " He let his voice trail off with an uncharacteristic tone, Daniel thought, suggesting enthusiasm for things left unsaid. Gerard picked up a clay pipe and began to fill the small bowl, watching Daniel and the pipe equally. After a moment of silence, Daniel spoke, but not in a manner to encourage the older man.

"My own time in London gave me an evil impression of that city," he said.

Gerard took a stick from the fire, touched the pipebowl and inhaled deeply. "Indeed, Daniel, indeed!" he said, "I am right glad to hear it." He exhaled smoke through his teeth.

"Let me tell you that my experience, limited though it was, but freer by a great deal than yours, caused me to be mightily afraid of the great scourge of that city, which we here have now so well left behind—thanks be to God! . . . I mean the pox, Daniel. The French disease."

Although he could see that this turn in the conversation made Daniel uncomfortable, Gerard pressed forward.

"What did I see, Daniel? I shall tell you—the visible, horrible mark of behavior usually invisible to other men, but horrible in the eyes of God and judged so on their bodies. So common was the pox in London that it seemed one man in every ten must be marked by it—and of course women of the worst kind were marked by it, too. I have seen men with pocks disfiguring all their visible flesh, and even those with their noses rotting away from the disease! Horrible, I say; horrible! You saw no worse in the English prison, I warrant you, eh?"

Daniel nodded without enthusiasm. He had expected this inquiry about the pox.

"Those with the pox usually do not get well, and they often die younger than they should, and painfully. And if they have children, they, too, often have the disease."

Gerard Spencer sat back in his chair, inhaling deeply on his pipe, so that his belly lifted. "God in his mercy has led me from such sin," he resumed, "and to father such children as He may be proud!" Gerard slapped the table with the large flat of his hand.

Daniel drew his breath at this outburst.

"You are a man of enough years that all this—the pox—you surely know." Spencer waved his hand, as if to put his exposition behind them.

"But you are also a man of enough years that it is possible that sometime in your past you have become infected. Perhaps during the war; perhaps otherwise; perhaps out of youthful ignorance—'tis common enough. This is the question a jealous father must ask."

As Daniel had listened to Mehitable's father, a red flush of discomfort slowly crossed from behind his neck to his brow, and as the other fell silent, he sat for a moment not speaking, with his ears and forehead colored, though whether by shame, embarrassment, or indignation the color alone did not communicate. After a long pause he began to speak.

"I understand that you are asking me a question—and are making no assumptions about the answer," he said, at length, with a subdued voice. "And I understand that a father must ask the question, for his child's sake."

The two men gave each other measured looks.

"With any other man," Daniel continued, "and with any other circumstance, I should have taken offense. But I want the same future for Mehitable, as do you. I am free of the pox. I have had nothing whatever to do with it!"

Gerard nodded seriously, came toward Daniel, and clapped him on both shoulders, breathing a sigh of relief. "I believe you, Daniel."

He held Daniel at arms' length. "I do, Daniel, but it is finally not I who must be satisfied, but God. I trust you will not take offense if I ask you to swear by this holy Bible."

"No offense," Daniel said, and put his hand on the outstretched book. "I swear that I have neither the infirmity known as the pox nor believe, in truth, that I have had any occasion to be so infected."

Gerard put the Bible down on the table and looked Daniel in the eye. "That is finished and never to be spoken of again."

Daniel sat quietly, waiting for the older man to break the silence. Gerard tapped the ashes out of his pipe.

"Now, shall we discuss the marriage contract?" he asked.

Samuel Wyllys knew very well how precarious the position of the Connecticut Colony still was. He held two recent letters from Governor Winthrop, written in England. For several months the Connecticut magistrates had awaited further notice of the progress of the governor's mission to secure a new charter from King Charles. It galled many of them, the Connecticut Puritans, that after the too-brief rule of the English Puritans under Cromwell, following the general's death it had not been long before a king was back on the throne, wielding the authority to replace the colony's government with one of his own choosing. A little decade, and the security of Puritan governance was gone! Connecticut had no certain legal status as a colony.

Still, Connecticut might continue to govern herself with a new charter endorsed by the king, and Winthrop had hurried off to England a full year before, entrusted with his anxious compatriots' hopes. Finally, the first of the letters Wyllys had opened, penned on May 14, 1662 by the governor, communicated Winthrop's great relief and satisfaction that the charter had been obtained, "so full and large in the grants and privileges therein." Winthrop had one copy, with the King's seal, sent by boat to the colony.

And then the second letter, written hastily only days later, communicated unexpected trouble: The ambassador for Rhode Island, seeking that colony's own charter, had challenged the terms of Connecticut's! Winthrop expressed concern but also his belief that Connecticut's friends in the court would lead ultimately to a confirmation of the charter. But it might take more time . . . weeks or even months.

Wyllys, as he sat in his father's study in Hartford, considered the import of the charter and the delay abroad, as he reflected on the situation at home. Connecticut Colony's neighbors, New London, New Haven, Rhode Island, and Massachusetts, all had their own colonists wishing to expand into territory as yet unsettled by colonists. At the margins between the colonies, a settlement could be a strong argument for expanding the power and influence of the colony.

Wyllys well recognized that Hartford's strategic position along the Connecticut River could be supported by additional settlements downriver toward the river's mouth, and so two years before, in October 1660, he had been party to the General Court's establishing a committee to acquire lands from the Indians. The settlement was to be in the vicinity of a large island in the river that the colonists called Thirty Mile Island. The acquisition was delayed, however, by more pressing affairs and by Governor Winthrop's departure for England in July 1661, but through the latter half of that year, Wyllys and Matthew Allyn, as members of the committee, had quietly gone about arranging the purchase from the local Indians.

Wyllys took pleasure in reading again the deed made to him:

Hartford, Feb. 20, 1662.
Know all men home hee presence may concerne that I Taukishe Sachem now wife to paux & Henumpam my daughter doe for our one selves our Heirs and assignes for and in Consideration of Three yeards of Tradinge cloth & Six fathom of Wompome etc. doe for ever Sell and make over all our right intrest & tittle unto thirtymile mile Iseland unto Samll Willys his heirs & assignes for ever The sd Taukishe and her daughter hereby declaringe Theire True right & Tittle unto the sd Iseland and hereby warantinge their sd tittle. . . .

In exchange for the cloth and wampum, Wyllys had received, on behalf of the colony, a large parcel of land stretching along the Connecticut River from the Mattabesick Mill River in the north to the lower end of the Pattaquonock Meadows in the south and extending six miles into the country on each side of the Great River.

To secure the new plantation for Connecticut, the colony needed new settlers. Now that the King's charter for Connecticut—that all-important sheet of parchment—had been received in September, Wyllys felt confident that the colony might proceed with the Thirty Mile Island plantation. Deliberately. Without haste. Wyllys knew that there was some risk of adjustment of the charter, but he had the greatest faith in the governor's abilities and felt quite sure that the colony's legal status would now endure. The plantation at Thirty Mile Island could go forward, at least in attracting prospective settlers for a later date. As to who they might be, Samuel Wyllys had some ideas.

"Goodman Spencer!" Samuel Wyllys called out from across the road.

The two men turned to him.

"Ah, of course, good day to you as well, Thomas!" said Wyllys, approaching the brothers as they stood outside Thomas Spencer's furniture shop. "I saw your brother," he said to Thomas, "and I wanted to compliment him."

"I have heard the happy news of your daughter being with child," said Wyllys to Gerard Spencer.

"Well met, sir," Gerard replied. "Yes, Mehitable and Daniel are very happy at God's grace. Thank you for your regard."

"It occurred to me, Ensign Spencer—it is 'Ensign,' is it not?—"

Gerard nodded.

"—that this child might suggest a new opportunity, if you'll permit me to explain."

Gerard nodded again and leaned his weight on his walking stick, preparing to listen.

"You have already been of good service to the community, I say, by investing so considerably in our town these last months."

Gerard Spencer cocked an eye at the younger man.

"Ah, do not fear, the details are unknown to me, nor should I wish to know them," Wyllys continued. "It is just widely appreciated that you have bought . . . several . . . parcels."

"Nine, as it happens," said Gerard, with a little emphasis.

"Nine, indeed, Ensign!" Wyllys seemed quite beside himself.

"Well, sir, they are not all of great size . . . nor, in truth, do I own them all outright—if you understand me."

"I do, sir."

Wyllys cleared his throat.

"Given your, shall we say, apparent interest in land, I wanted you to know of a most excellent opportunity."

"Pray, sir, I am listening."

"On behalf of the colony, I have acquired a substantial tract along the river south of here, which we purpose to divide into some twenty or so home lots, in very favorable positions. Good soils, fronting the river. The river is teeming with salmon there."

"What is this plantation to be called?" asked Gerard.

"Thirty Mile Island, for the island in the river there."

Gerard Spencer tapped his walking stick on the ground and kept his eyes averted for a moment. When he raised them again they held the look of a man commencing to trade.

"Well, sir, you have gained my interest. It is true; Mehitable and Daniel are at the point of starting a family. My son, John, is also at that age. As a father, I can think of no finer gift to them than to have their own lands and opportunity.

"A happy thought, Ensign. A generous thought!"

"Generous, aye,—if and I can afford it, Mr. Wyllys!" Gerard let out a great merry laugh. "Who knows, perhaps all the Spencers should move to this plantation—under the right terms."

"Well, we shall speak again of this another time?"

"Indeed, sir! You have gained my interest."

Samuel Wyllys bade the Spencer brothers good morning and moved away down the path. After a time he allowed himself a broad smile and chuckle as he considered how the interests of individuals and their community could be made so agreeable.

Afterward: Proprietor, Freeman, Father

D aniel Cone lived for four decades beyond his separation from John Winthrop, Jr. Those decades can be imagined as full of the challenges and rewards of making a home in an unfamiliar wilderness, as Daniel settled along the Connecticut River and raised a family.

After Daniel married Mehitable in 1662, the next year brought the first of nine children. Over the next 20 years, they had six sons and three daughters. As well as is known, five sons survived to marrying age, married, and had their own children (rapidly populating the plantation with Cones). The essential vital statistics that are readily available follow:

> *Ruth*, born 7 Jan. 1663; place of birth unknown
> *Hannah*, born 6 April 1664, by some accounts in Haddam
>   —*Remaining children all born in Haddam*—
> *Daniel*, born 21 Jan 1666, married Mary Gates, died 15 June
>   1725.
> *Jared*, born 7 Jan 1668, married Elizabeth——, died
>   11 April 1711.
> *Rebecca*, born 6 Feb. 1670.
> *Ebenezer*, baptized 25 March 1673.
> *Nathaniel*, baptized 6 June 1675, married Sarah Hungerford,
>   died about 1730.
> *Stephen*, baptized 26 March 1678, married Mary
>   Hungerford, died 1 Dec. 1756.
> *Caleb*, baptized 19 March 1682, married Elizabeth
>   Cunningham, died 25 Sept. 1743.

Daniel's father-in-law, Gerard Spencer, did indeed act on the opportunity to settle his family in the new plantation at Thirty Mile Island. Not only was Gerard one of the original settlers and landholders (so-called "proprietors"), so also were Gerard's eldest son, John; Daniel Cone, married to Gerard's eldest daughter; and Daniel Brainerd, married to Gerard's next-oldest daughter, Hannah.

What role, if any, Gerard played in financially assisting either son-in-law, or son, in becoming Haddam proprietors is not known. According to the first list of 29 proprietors, dated October 27, 1665, the value of the estates of the men were markedly different; the value of Daniel Cone and Daniel Brainerd were 74 and 76 pounds, respectively, and John Spencer, 81 pounds, while Gerard Spencer's value was 219 pounds, making him the second-wealthiest among the heads of households.

The average valuation for all 29 listed men was 107 pounds, so Gerard's relations were among the less well-off, at least by this valuation. However, the value in currency would not have been the only measure of a plantation proprietor's material wealth or economic well-being. In an agricultural and fishing economy, barter was the basis of most transactions, and in this, a family's industry could generate commodities—be they fruit, grain, or fish—that would be both valuable in trade and support a quality of life quite independent of an individual's net worth in currency. (What exactly was counted in these 1665 proprietor valuations is also not definitely known, nor is the monetary standard certain, though a rough comparison may be drawn from knowing that a bushel of wheat earlier that decade in Connecticut was valued at 3.5 shillings. Twenty shillings equaled one pound.)

When exactly the men settled the plantation is also debated. While tradition and even some modern accounts indicate that the settlement occurred within a year of Samuel Wyllys's acquisition of title from the Indians or "immediately after the royal charter was issued"—that is, in 1662 or 1663—Haddam was probably not settled until later, in spring 1665. The families would have waited until spring to give them the greatest amount of time to establish homes and crops before the onset of winter.

What, then, was happening to Daniel and Mehitable in 1663 and 1664? Daniel was probably employed, earning enough from his work to have attained the 1665 valuation of his estate noted on the proprietors' list. Mehitable was caring for one infant and by early fall 1663 was pregnant again. They were very likely living in Hartford, perhaps on one of the home sites that Gerard purchased from those religious conservatives who moved away.

Under the circumstances of his recent marriage and relatively recent entry into the labor market as a free agent, it's quite possible that Daniel was employed by a member of his new in-laws' family. Thomas Spencer, as a longtime resident of Hartford and merchant furniture-maker, would have been more likely than father-in-law Gerard to have been that employer. If he worked for Thomas, it's possible that Daniel would have contributed to the making of the ceremonial chair presented to Governor Winthrop in 1663 in celebration on his return home from the successful mission to obtain a charter for the colony. Such an occasion would have been a fine moment for celebration of life's progress, for both Winthrop and Daniel.

Two court cases give other glimpses of Daniel's life in those two years. He was a defendant in a case heard March 1663, charged by a Mrs. Mary Skreech with owing her a "debt with damadge" for almost three pounds. The outcome of the case is not known, but some details are of interest. Mrs. Skreech was represented by attorney Nicholas Varlet, who was Dutch, suggesting that she may have been Dutch as well, and that Daniel may have continued to have some contact with the New York Dutch, perhaps through connections established when serving John Winthrop (who, as his intercession with Governor Stuyvesant on Daniel's behalf had previously shown, was certainly connected at the highest levels of society). In any event, Daniel knew Mrs. Skreech well enough to borrow from her.

On the same court docket as the complaint against Daniel, Mary Skreech made two other claims of "debt with damadge" against another man, Peter Grant. The linking of Daniel and Peter may be more than coincidental. Grant was also a Scot, and very likely the same Peter Grant who worked at both the Great Works in the north woods and at the Saugus Ironworks in the Bay Colony. If indeed Daniel and Peter were acquaintances, or more—as the court case would imply—such a relationship supports the interpretation that Daniel also worked at one or both of these places.

In 1664, Daniel was again involved in a court case in Hartford. Earlier, Daniel and a Mr. Lord had disputed who owned a steer. At trial, the jury was undecided. The court advised the parties to either divide the steer between them or continue the case in the General Court. The latter was apparently done, and the court minutes of the October 13, 1664 session at Hartford (Governor Winthrop, presiding) show the verdict against Daniel:

> The Court appoynted Mr. Campfeild, Deacon More, Mr. Fayrechild, Mr. Hull and Lnt Olmsteed, as a Committee to ripen the busines respecting the calfe in controuersie between Mr. Lord and Danll Cone, whoe returne that they haueing veiwed the sayd beast and the evidences of both sides, doe iudge it to be Mr. Lord's steare. The

Court confirmes this yr determination that the stear doth belong to Mr. Lord.

It seems almost certain that Daniel would have been living in Hartford in the fall of 1664, as the court document notes that the committee "viewed the

sayd beast" and it seems very unlikely that several men would have undertaken a lengthy journey to and from the Thirty Mile Island plantation to adjudicate so minor a case. Moreover, no "Lord" is listed on the 1665 list of original proprietors there, and the Mr. Lord in question appears to be Capt. Richard Lord, often cited in the records of Connecticut Colony and a resident of Hartford.

What else may this case yield? It is impossible to know the merits of the claims of ownership, of course, but it is worth noting that Mr. Lord was a notable of the community, and the committee hearing the controversy included three other gentlemen, a church deacon, and a lieutenant in the militia (one may hope he was not the immediate inferior of Capt. Lord). Whether the social status of the parties played any overt role in the decision can not be known, although it is certainly fair to consider. In any case, the fact that Daniel was able to plausibly claim ownership of a steer suggests that he was

The "Joined Great Chair," believed to have been presented to Governor Winthrop, features turned legs and armrest posts reputedly made by Thomas Spencer.

living in such circumstances that would have permitted husbandry of the animal–living on a farm or at least on enough land to support the growing animal.

Beginning probably in 1662, the colony's committee, headed by Wyllys, had divided the best land of the plantation along the west side of the Connecticut river into 30 home lots of seven or eight acres each and began to sell them. Two lots were dedicated for a blacksmith and minister, the other 28 were presumably offered to any interested party. By the spring of 1665, 27 lots had been sold, and around two dozen men, their wives, and their children moved from Hartford and nearby towns to settle the plantation.

Only a little is known about most of the men, but one common feature of interest is that at least seven of them, including Daniel, had previously been servants, apprentices, or wards of prosperous colonists. "This circumstance," observed town historian Francis Parker, "is not to be taken as meaning that they were not of goodly origin and honorable birth, but it is proof conclusive that they had not the advantage of wealth, and that the burden of making their own way in the Connecticut wilderness rested upon themselves."

Daniel's homestead was about in the middle of the 19 lots that comprised the northern section of the town settlement; a second smaller settlement to the south contained the remaining lots. Like most of the others', Daniel's lot ran roughly northeast to southwest and was narrow north and south but stretched generously from its front on the Connecticut river west into somewhat more upland acreage. Four acres of the lots were to the east of a highway that divided the lots; about three acres were to the west of it. The first homes were supposedly built on the river side but close to this highway running between Hartford and the coast. Such a location would have had several advantages: proximity to neighbors and the attendant security; access to the highway; a convenient east-west midpoint in the individual properties; and direct access to the river bottom land that was best for growing crops. In addition, the nearby river frontage would have also provided access to fish, including seasonal runs of salmon.

Daniel's lot was just south of his brother-in-law Brainerd's; father-in-law Gerard was three lots further north; and Gerard's son, John, was near the northern edge of the settlement. In time Daniel would acquire another lot, originally dedicated to the blacksmith.

It is hard to imagine all the challenges that Daniel and his fellow settlers would have encountered in constructing homes, clearing and preparing fields, planting annual crops and perennial fruit trees, tending livestock, and raising young children, but they were no doubt fully occupied in a way that may be hard for modern Americans to imagine. At least the settlers seem to have had no serious conflicts with the local native tribes from whom they had acquired their land, though it does seem quite likely that some tension over time must have arisen from competition over wild game and fish. Salmon, abundant in those days, was no doubt a welcome source of protein for both native and settler, and it is said that the settlers used seines to catch them, presumably in some quantity.

One significant moment in Daniel's life in the early years following settlement occurred at a court of election held at Hartford, May 13, 1669. At this session John Winthrop, Jr., was again elected governor of Connecticut, and several men of the plantation, now called Haddam, were "presented for freemen" and duly recorded, including "Mr.

The Connecticut River frontage of Daniel Cone's original Haddam homesite (lower) has returned to a vegetated state as part of a state park. The East Haddam shore is readily visible across the river.

Nicho: Noices, John Spencer, Danll Braynard, Joseph Stonard, DanllCone, Mr. Bates, James Wells, and Richard Pyper." What a moment of pride this would have been for Daniel, to have been made a freeman (a status which didn't signify a release from bondage but instead a full investiture into colonial society). To become a freeman meant that you had enough property, had received a certificate from those in authority in your town that you were peaceable and of "honest conversation," and had given an oath of fidelity to Jesus Christ and to the colony. In return, a freeman could participate in elections for the colony's leadership, the General Assembly. Although becoming a freeman was not exactly rare in Connecticut in the 1660s, achieving the status would have marked yet another milestone in the progress of Daniel Cone—and, importantly—one witnessed and confirmed by his former master.

Daniel was a commissioner for the town of Haddam in 1669, but for most of the next ten years the specific activities of Daniel are not known. He is said to have "become one of the most important men in the new town," holding "town offices" and in later years being listed as one of the five

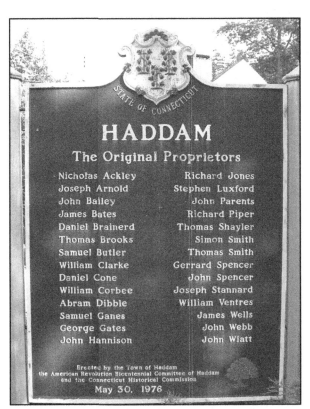

proprietors of Haddam in the town patent (an official certification) in 1687. As late as 1703, when he is about 77 years old, colony court records list him, as *Mr.* Daniel Cone, as an "agent for the town of Haddam" in a dispute with the town of Saybrook.

As court records maddeningly do, brief and curious mentions of Daniel also tell something of his more private affairs —*something*, but not so much as to take great meanings from it. In 1674, Thomas

Smith, Daniel's near neighbor, made a last will, in which he gave his "turnips equally betwixt James Welles, Daniel Cone, Joseph Stennard and John Bailey." (One can only hope there were a good number of turnips.) Further, Smith bequeathed "what Timothy Spencer oweth me to Daniel Cone"—an unspecified amount.

The years 1675 and 1676 were tumultuous for New England, as the region was embattled in King Philip's War, the major war with several New England tribes, led by Metacomet, known to the English as Philip. The towns of the Connecticut Colony made allies of some local tribes, offering bounties against "our common enemy." While the towns of the colony did not suffer attacks as many in Massachusetts and Rhode Island did, Connecticut sent its militias to fight alongside its neighbors. Over 100 Connecticut militia were killed out of approximately 800 colonists who died. Gerard Spencer was an ensign in the Haddam militia, but no record of him or his sons is found among the list of combatants. Friction among the colonies ultimately stopped the actions of their militias but not before the tribes, particularly the Narragansetts, suffered severe losses. At war's end the enemy tribes had lost an estimated 3,000 individuals. They were never a substantial threat again.

The 1680s, the decade of Daniel's mid-fifties to mid-sixties, left several documents of interest. In 1682, when Daniel was 56 years old, his last child, Caleb, was born, giving Daniel's father-in-law the pleasure of knowing all his Cone grandchildren before the end of his own life. For in 1685 Gerard Spencer passed away, leaving a last will that gave particular notice and equal familial rights to Daniel and his children: "It is my Will that my son John Spencer his Children and my son-in-law Daniel Cone his Children have an equal proportion of my Estate with my other Children."

In about that same year, or perhaps as early as 1683, Daniel and his family moved across the Connecticut River to establish a new settlement, soon known as East Haddam. "It is probable that he was the first of the original proprietors to remove [from Haddam] and that his dwelling house was the first erected at the Creek Row," that is, along a nearby creek that ran into the Connecticut River (at the time still called the Great River). Where the original home site was is not completely clear, but one historic account places the Cone home and those of members of the Gates, Bates, and Brainerd families on the hillside below the northern limit of East Haddam and just above the Salmon River, where they could look across the Great River and see the Haddam homesites. What caused the early East Haddam settlers to move there is unclear. Perhaps it was just the emerging American appetite for more space.

Curiously, in 1689 Daniel was relieved of the obligation of paying personal taxes, although whether that was due to some conspicuous service to the colony, some privilege of seniority, or some other reason, is unknown. That he was active on behalf of his community has been mentioned. Daniel was involved, as nearly all his contemporaries were also, in church life, but as an elder of the town he was even more active, serving as a founding member of the First Church of Christ in East Haddam in 1704. The establishment of that church on the east side of the river brought a definite division between the two Haddam communities and separated the east side from a somewhat checkered history in Haddam with its ministers, who included Nicholas Noyes. Noyes, who lived among Daniel and his neighbors for some 15 years, afterwards went to Salem, where he helped prosecute the infamous witchcraft trials of 1692.

Daniel, as a church elder, at some point is likely to have had to give evidence, in church, of a spiritual conversion to the orthodoxies of the Puritan "Congregational" faith, as it was then practiced. Noteworthy in terms of the family's likely orthodoxy is that Daniel Cone, Jr., was chosen as one of the first two deacons of that first East Haddam church.

Mehitable died in 1691, and the year later Daniel married Rebecca, the widow of Richard Walkley of Haddam. Little about her, including her maiden name, is known, but she was considerably Daniel's junior—which would probably have been a benefit to Daniel, then in his later sixties, as he still had three boys (two teenagers and a 10-year-old) to raise. Daniel retained ownership of lands in Haddam and supposedly returned there to live about 1695, although it may be he lived in both towns, off and on. A ferry ran between the towns starting in 1695.

The last document of Daniel's life is also the only, apparently, in his own words—a deed conveying his Haddam property to his youngest son, Caleb, then 24 years old. Composed October 7, 1706, seventeen days before he died, it summarizes the property Daniel owned in Haddam at the time and bequeaths ownership of home, other buildings, and fruit trees. It also gives, in one short phrase describing Caleb, a brief glimpse of the values of the man and the character of his son—"my well-beloved and dutiful son":

> For and in the consideration of love and good-will and
> affection which I bear and have to and for my well-beloved and
> dutiful son, Caleb Cone, have given and granted, by these presents

freely, clearly and absolutely give and grant to the said Caleb Cone, his heirs, executors, etc., my dwelling house, with two allotments joining thereto, with all the fruit trees and buildings I have upon, with all the appurtenances and privileges as I hold unto, which lots contain five acres; and a lot that was John Blackford's in the home field lying between the lot of Mr. Nicholas Noyes and a lot of Thomas Brooks, which lot is eight rods wide and length from the Great River to the country road, and my lower division or lot at lower end of meadow, which contains in measure three acres and a half, with one acre I bought of Samuel Spencer, which acre is adjoining to the above three acres and a half. . . .

To whom his property in East Haddam was given or willed is not certain, but Daniel's son Stephen inherited it eventually and passed it on to his sons, and it stayed in the family for many years. In 1871, a local historian

In 2005, the headstone was still legible of the earliest-known Cone grave in Haddam's Burial Yard of the Thirty Mile Island Plantation, established in 1667. It is that of Daniel's youngest son (and the author's ancestor), Caleb. The headstone is inscribed: "Here lies Interr[ed]/ the Body of Cap[t.]/ Caleb Cone who/ died Sept. [25, 1743]."

wrote that the East Haddam farm originally settled by Daniel was "recently purchased from Jonathan Cone by Benjamin Edwards. Until this transfer it has remained in the Cone family."

Even so, by the late 1800s many Cones had left Haddam and East Haddam to seek their fortunes elsewhere. Writing in 1903, family chronicler William Whitney Cone documented the lives of more than 6,500 Cone descendants in North America, a listing which he lamented was incomplete. The fates of all have been known best by their closest relatives, of course, but one thing can be said of all of them: they can trace their origin to a man named Daniel.

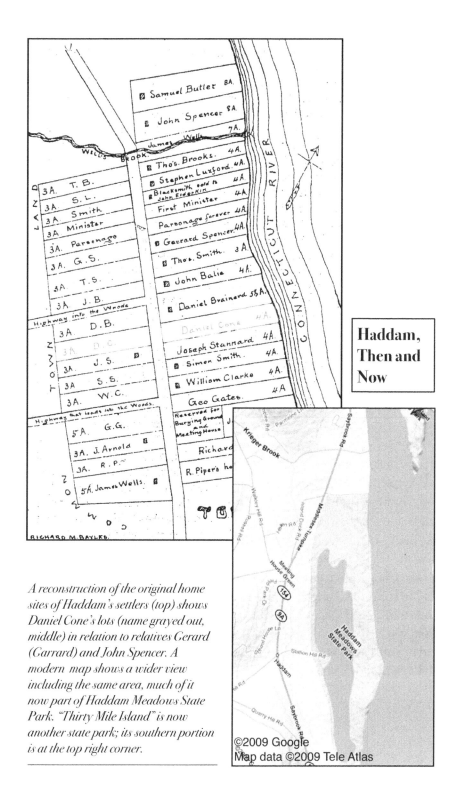

A reconstruction of the original home sites of Haddam's settlers (top) shows Daniel Cone's lots (name grayed out, middle) in relation to relatives Gerard (Garrard) and John Spencer. A modern map shows a wider view including the same area, much of it now part of Haddam Meadows State Park. "Thirty Mile Island" is now another state park; its southern portion is at the top right corner.

Appendix: A Few Notes on the Name "Cone"

The U. S. Census publishes a list of frequencies of last names in America. The last currently available accounting, the 2000 census, shows Cone ranked 3,337 out of more than 150,000 unique last names in a population of more than 271 million Americans. The 2000 census counted 9,824 Cones (88 percent of whom were non-Hispanic whites). For comparison, there were slightly more Cohns (9,859) and fewer Sanborns (9,750) and just as many Henriquezes. Calhoun, the most common Americanized version of the clan (Colquhoun) name, ranked considerably higher in frequency at 758, with 41,452 individuals counted.

    While the *John and Sara*'s ship passenger's list refers to a Daniel MacHoe, if Daniel Cone's original Scottish name was the more likely MacCone, there were indeed Scots with that spelling recorded from 1497. The standard source on Scottish names references that spelling as an Anglicizing of MacEoghain (MacEwan). "Mac" itself is a Gaelic prefix occurring in Scottish names of Gaelic origin, and means "son."

    As Daniel appears to have spelled his name "Conn" in the only known document in which he signs his name, it can't be ruled out that his name was, or was originally, "Conn." *Surnames of Scotland* tells that Conn is "an old name in Aberdeenshire, where there was a prominent Roman Catholic family of the name, Cone or Cone of Auchry [who] claimed to be a branch of the Clan Donald, the surname being assumed from the traditional name of the Clan, 'Siol Cuin,' or 'Con.'" A George Con was the Pope's agent at the court of Charles I during 1636-39 and "the family was driven into exile soon after 1642," the year in which the Civil Wars began. Driven into exile from where to where is not clear from this account, although since this Con had Royalist sympathies, it would seem unlikely that exile would have been to Puritan New England.

Bibliography

Anderson, William. *The Scottish Nation: Or, the Surnames, Families, Literature, Honours, and Biographical History of the People of Scotland.* Edinburgh: A. Fullarton & Co., 1862.

Andrews, Charles McLean. "The Beginnings of the Connecticut Towns." *Annals of the American Academy of Political and Social Science* I, (1890): 165-91.

——. *The Beginnings of Connecticut, 1632-1662.* Edited by Committee on Historical Publications Tercentenary Commission of the State of Connecticut. New Haven: Published for the Tercentenary Commission by the Yale University Press, 1934.

Aronson, Marc. *John Winthrop, Oliver Cromwell, and the Land of Promise.* New York: Clarion Books, 2004.

Atkin, Malcolm. *Cromwell's Crowning Mercy: The Battle of Worcester 1651.* Stroud, Gloucestershire: Sutton, 1998.

Banks, Charles Edward. "Scotch Prisoners Deported to New England by Cromwell, 1651-52." *Massachusetts Historical Society Proceedings* LXI (1927): 4-29.

Bayles, Richard W. "Town of Haddam." In *History of Middlesex County, Connecticut, 1635 to 1885,* edited by J. B. Beers. New York: J. B. Beers and Co., 1884.

Bell, Dennis. "Battle of Dunbar, 1650." ScotWars, http://www.scotwars.com/html/battle_of_dunbar.htm.

Black, George Fraser. *The Surnames of Scotland; Their Origin, Meaning, and History.* New York: New York Public Library, 1946.

Black, Robert C. *The Younger John Winthrop.* New York: Columbia University Press, 1966.

Blood, Peter E. "Biographical Sketch of Gerard Spencer." www.familyorigins.com/users/b/l/o/Peter-E-Blood/FAMO5-0001/d56.htm#P1316

Bowden, Henry Warner. "Puritanism, Puritans." BELIEVE Religious Information Source web-site, http://mb-soft.com/believe/txc/puritani.htm.

Bozeman, Theodore Dwight. *To Live Ancient Lives: The Primitivist Dimension in Puritanism.* Chapel Hill: Published for the Institute of

Early American History and Culture, Williamsburg, Virginia, by the University of North Carolina Press, 1988.

Bremer, Francis J. *John Winthrop: America's Forgotten Founding Father*. New York: Oxford University Press, 2003.

Bushman, Richard L. *From Puritan to Yankee; Character and the Social Order in Connecticut, 1690-1765*. Cambridge: Harvard University Press, 1967.

Caldwell, Patricia. *The Puritan Conversion Narrative: The Beginnings of American Expression*. Cambridge: Cambridge University Press, 1983.

Carlson, Steven. "The Saugus Iron Works." http://members.tripod.com/graytim/Saugus.htm

Carlton, William R. "Overland to Connecticut in 1645: A Travel Diary of John Winthrop." *New England Quarterly* 13, (1940): 494-510.

Chase, Levi Badger. *The Bay Path and Along the Way*. Norwood, Mass.: The Plimpton Press, 1919.

Cone, William Whitney. *Some Account of the Cone Family in America: Principally of the Descendants of Daniel Cone, Who Settled in Haddam, Connecticut in 1662*. Topeka, Kansas: Crane & Co., 1903.

Connecticut Colony. *The Public Records of the Colony of Connecticut, from April 1636 to October 1776*. 15 vols. Hartford: Brown and Parsons, 1850-1890.

Cunningham, Janice P., and Elizabeth A. Warner. *Portrait of a River Town*. Middletown, Conn.: Greater Middletown Preservation Trust, 1994.

Davenport, John. "God's Call to His People to Turn Unto Him; Together with His Promise to Turn Unto Them." In *Early American imprints. 1st series; no. 137*. Cambridge [Mass.]: Printed by S.G. [Samuel Green] and M.J. [Marmaduke Johnson] for John Usher of Boston, 1669.

Demos, John. *Entertaining Satan: Witchcraft and the Culture of Early New England*. New York: Oxford University Press, 1982.

Dobson, David. *Dictionary of Scots Banished to the American Plantations, 1650-1775*. Baltimore: Genealogical Publishing Co., 1983.

Dow, George Francis. *The Historical Collections of the Topsfield Historical Society*. Topsfied, Mass.: Topsfield Historical Society, 1895.

Dunn, Richard S. *Puritans and Yankees: The Winthrop Dynasty of New England, 1630-1717*. Princeton, N.J.: Princeton University Press, 1962.

Evelyn, John. *Sylva, or a Discourse of Forest Trees*. 4th ed.1706. Reprint, London: Doubleday & Co. 1908.

Fabricius, Johannes. *Syphilis in Shakespeare's England*. London; Bristol, Penn.: Jessica Kingsley, 1994.

Felch, William Farrand, George C. Atwell, H. Phelps Arms, and Francis Trevelyan Miller. *The Connecticut magazine*. (1845).

Field, David D. *A History of the Towns of Haddam and East-Haddam*. Middletown, Conn.: Loomis and Richards, 1814.

First Church of Christ. *Historical Catalogue of the First Church in Hartford, 1633-1885*. Hartford: Pub. by the Church, 1885.

Fowler, David H. "Connecticut's Freemen: The First Forty Years." *The William and Mary Quarterly* 3rd Ser., Vol. 15, no. 3 (1958): 312-33.

Friedlander, Mary Banning "My American Heritage: Chapter Two, the Tanner Line." http://freepages.genealogy.rootsweb.com/~mbfriedlander/tanner.html

Galenson, David W. *White Servitude in Colonial America: An Economic Analysis*. Cambridge: Cambridge University Press, 1981.

Games, Alison. *Migration and the Origins of the English Atlantic World*. Vol. 133, Harvard Historical Studies. Cambridge, MA: Harvard University Press, 2001.

Gardiner, Lion, and W. Dodge. *A History of the Pequot War, or, a Relation of the War between the Powerful Nation of Pequot Indians, Once Inhabiting the Coast of New-England, Westerly from near Narraganset Bay and the English Inhabitants, in the Year 1638*. Cincinnati: Printed by J. Harpel for W. Dodge, 1860.

Gehring, Charles T., and Peter Stuyvesant. *Correspondence, 1654-1658*. Syracuse, N.Y.: Syracuse University Press, 2003.

Greene, M. Louise. *The Development of Religious Liberty in Connecticut*. Boston and New York: Houghton, Mifflin and Co., 1905. Reprint, Project Gutenberg.

Greubel, Rand. "Who Was John Sinkler?" http://kingcrest.com/sinclair/johnsinkler.html-ssi.

Hartley, E. N. *Ironworks on the Saugus*. Norman, OK: University of Oklahoma Press, 1957.

Haynes, George Henry. "The Tale of Tantiusques: An Early Mining Venture in Massachusetts." *American Antiquarian Society Proceedings* 14, (1902): 471-97.

Hinman, R. R. *A Catalogue of the Names of the First Puritan Settlers of the Colony of Connecticut*. Hartford: Printed by E. Gleason, 1846.

Hodges, Miles. "Our Story—Material for a Confirmation Class; Chapter 22. The Wars of Religion (1600s)." New Geneva Center, http://www.newgenevacenter.org/our-story/contents.htm.

Hood, J. Edward, and Donald Weinhardt. "Working the Sturbridge Graphite Mine (Part Ii) " Old Sturbridge Inc., http://www.osv.org/learning/DocumentViewer.php?pf=Y&Action=View&DocID=627.

Hooker, Thomas. "Rev. Thomas Hooker's Letter, in Reply to Governor Winthrop." *Collections of the Connecticut Historical Society*. (1860), http://www.archive.org/details/revthomashookers00hookrich.

Innes, Stephen. *Creating the Commonwealth: The Economic Culture of Puritan New England*. New York: W. W. Norton & Co., 1995.

Jernagan, Marcus. "The Economic and Social Influence of the Indentured Servant." In *The Underside of American History*, edited by Thomas R. Frazier, 59-72. New York: Harcourt Brace Javonovich, 1971.

Johnson, Claudia D. *Daily Life in Colonial New England*. Wesport, Conn.: Greenwood Press, 2002.

Jordan, Winthrop D. "The Beginnings of Slavery in North America." In *The Underside of American History*, edited by Thomas R. Frazier, 30-58. New York: Harcourt Brace Javonovich, 1971.

Kamil, Neil. *Fortress of the Soul: Violence, Metaphysics, and Material Life in the Huguenots' New World, 1517-1751*. Baltimore: Johns Hopkins University Press, 2005.

Lewis, Alonzo. *The History of Lynn, Including Nahant*. Lynn, Mass.: S. M. Dickinson, 1844.

Love, William DeLoss *The Colonial History of Hartford*. Hartford, Conn.: Centinel Hill Press, 1914. Reprint, 1974.

Mackenzie, George N. *Colonial Families of the United States of America*. 7 vols. Baltimore: Genealogical Publishing Co., 1912. Reprint, 1995.

Manwaring, Charles William. *A Digest of the Early Connecticut Probate Records*. Baltimore: Genealogical Publishing Co., Inc., 1995.

Massachusetts Historical Society. *Winthrop Papers*. Edited by Adam Winthrop, John Winthrop, John Winthrop, Fitz-John Winthrop,

Wait Still Winthrop and Massachusetts Historical Society. Boston: Massachusetts Historical Society, 1929.

——. *Winthrop Papers*. Edited by Malcolm Freiberg. Vol. VI, 1650-1654. Boston: Mass. Historical Society, 1992.

Miller, Perry, and Thomas Herbert Johnson. *The Puritans*. New York: American Book Co., 1938.

Morgan, Edmund S. *The Puritan Family: Essays on Religion and Domestic Relations in Seventeenth-Century New England*. 2nd ed. Boston: Trustees of the Public LIbrary, 1956.

Morgan, Kenneth. *Slavery and Servitude in Colonial North America: A Short History*. Washington Square, N.Y.: New York University Press, 2001.

Morris, Myrtle Melona. "Joseph and Philena (Elton) Fellows, and Their Ancestry and Descendants; Also the Ancestry of Reuben Fairchild, John and Dorothy (Waldorf) Turner and George Morris." http://www.geocities.com/Heartland/Prairie/5832/colonialfellows.htm.

National Park Service. "Saugus Iron Works–Reading 2." National Park Service, http://www.cr.nps.gov/nr/twhp/wwwlps/lessons/30saugus/30facts2.htm.

New England Historic Genealogical Society. "Scotch Prisoners Sent to Massachusettes in 1652 by Order of the English Government." In *New England Historical and Genealogical Register*, 377-80. Boston: New England Historic Genealogical Society, 1847.

Orr, Charles (ed.). *History of the Pequot War: The Contemporary Accounts of Mason, Underhill, Vincent and Gardener*. Cleveland: Helman-Taylor, 1897.

Osterweis, Rollin G. *Three Centuries of New Haven, 1638-1938*. New Haven: Yale University Press, 1953.

Parker, Francis Hubert. *Contributions to the History of East Haddam, Connecticut*. Hartford, Conn.: Connecticut State Library, 1938.

Parthesius, Robert, et al. "17th Century Galleys & the *Avondster*'s Fitted Kitchen." Maritime Archaeology Unit of Sri Lanka, http://cf.hum.uva.nl/galle/avondster/galley.html.

Pirsig, W. "Why Berwick?" http://www.obhs.net/WhyBerwick.html.

Pynchon, John. *The Pynchon Papers*. Edited by Carl Bridenbaugh and Juliette Tomlinson. Boston: Colonial Society of Massachusetts; Distributed by the University Press of Virginia, 1982.

——. *The Pynchon Papers: Selections from the Account Books of John Pynchon, 1651-1697*. Edited by Carl Bridenbaugh, and Juliette Tomlinson. Vol. 2. Boston: The Colonial Society of Massachusetts, 1985.

Rapaport, Diane. *New England Court Records: A Research Guide for Genealogists and Historians*. Burlington, Mass.: Quill Pen Press, 2006.

——. "Scots for Sale, Part 2." *New England Ancestors* (Holiday 2004): 26-28.

——. "Scots for Sale: The Fate of the Scottish Prisoners in Seventeenth-Century Massachusetts." *New England Ancestors* (Winter 2003).

Savage, James. *A Genealogical Dictionary of the First Settlers of New England, Showing Three Generations of Those Who Came before May 1692*. Vol. IV. Baltimore: Genealogical Pub Co., 1977.

Schama, Simon, et al. "Food on Board Dutch Ships in the 17th Century." http://www.olivetreegenealogy.com/nn/mm_10.shtml.

Sehr, Timothy J. *Colony and Commonwealth: Massachusetts Bay, 1649-1660*. New York: Garland Pub., 1989.

Shepard, Thomas. "The Autobiography of Thomas Shepard." In *The Literatures of Colonial America: An Anthology*, edited by Susan P. Castillo and Ivy Schweitzer, 278-80. Malden, Mass.: Blackwell, 2001.

Smith, Joseph Henry. *Colonial Justice in Western Massachusetts, 1639-1702; the Pynchon Court Record, an Original Judges' Diary of the Administration of Justice in the Springfield Courts in the Massachusetts Bay Colony*. Edited by Joseph Henry Smith. Cambridge, Mass.: Harvard University Press, 1961.

Spencer, Jack Taif, and Edith Wooley Spencer. *The Spencers of the Great Migration*. 2 vols. Vol. 1. Baltimore: Gateway Press, 1997.

Spencer, William Henry. *Spencer Family Record of the Springfield, Vt. And Evansville, Wisc. Descendants of Garrard Spencer of Haddam, Conn., Emigrant of 1630*. New York: Tobias A. Wright, 1907.

Stackpole, Everett. *History of New Hampshire*. 5 vols. New York: American Historical Society, 1916.

Stackpole, Everett and Lucien Thompson. *History of the Town of Durham, New Hampshire (Oyster River Plantation)*. 2 vols. Vol. 1. Concord, N.H.: Rumford Press, 1913.

Stofko, Karl P., and Rachel I. Gibbs. "A Brief History of East Haddam, Connecticut." In *Reprint of the Introduction to "A survey of the architectural and historical resources of the town of East Haddam," published in Dec. 1977 by the East Haddam Historic District Commission*. East Haddam, Conn.: Unknown, ca. 1977.

Sugar, Max. *Regional Identity and Behavior*. New York: Kluwer Academic/ Plenum Publishers, 2002.

Talpalar, Morris. *The Sociology of the Bay Colony*. New York: Philosophical Library, 1976.

Taylor, John M. *The Witchcraft Delusion in Colonial Connecticut*. Williamstown, Mass.: Corner House, 1908. Reprint, 1984.

Taylor, Norris. "The Spencer Family: Lynn, Mass. to Connecticut." http:// ntgen.tripod.com/bw/sp_bros.html.

Taylor, Robert Joseph. *Colonial Connecticut: A History*. Millwood, N.Y.: KTO Press, 1979.

The Trustees of Reservations. "Tantiusques: Property Description." http://www.thetrustees.org/pages/368_tantiusques.cfm.

Tomlinson, R.G. *Witchcraft Trials of Connecticut: The First Comprehensive, Documented History of Witchcraft Trials in Colonial Connecticut*. Hartford, Conn.: The Bond Press, 1978.

Trent, Robert F. "Coastal Algonkian Culture 1500-1680: Conquest and Resistance." In *New England Begins: The Seventeenth Century*, 66-71. Boston: Museum of Fine Arts, 1982.

——. "The Spencer Chairs and Regional Chairmaking in the Connecticut River Valley, 1639-1863." *Connecticut Historical Society Bulletin* 49, no. 4 (1984).

Trumbull, J. Hammond. *The Public Records of the Colony of Connecticut, Prior to the Union with New Haven Colony, May 1665*. Hartford, Conn.: Brown and Parsons, 1850.

Trumbull, J. Hammond, and Charles J. Hoadly. *The Public Records of the Colony of Connecticut [1636-1776]*. Hartford: Lockwood & Brainard Co., 1850.

Van Dusen, Albert E. *Puritans against the Wilderness: Connecticut History to 1763*. Chester, Conn.: Pequot Press, 1975.

Volo, James M., and Dorothy D. Volo. *Family Life in 17th- and 18th-Century America*. Westport, Conn.: Greenwood Press, 2006.

Wagner, David R., and Jack Dempsey. *Mystic Fiasco: How the Indians Won the Pequot War*. [Unknown city] Digital Scanning, Inc., 2003.

Walker, Alice Morehouse. *Historic Hadley*. New York: Grafton Press, 1906.

Waters, Thomas Franklin. *A Sketch of the Life of John Winthrop the Younger*. Vol. VII, Publications of the Ipswich Historical Society. Cambridge, Mass.: University Press, 1899.

Waters, Thomas Franklin, and Robert Charles Winthrop. *A Sketch of the Life of John Winthrop, the Younger: Founder of Ipswich, Massachusetts, in 1633*. Cambridge, Mass: J. Wilson and Son, 1899.

Wertenbaker, Thomas Jefferson. *The Puritan Oligarchy; the Founding of American Civilization*. New York: C. Scribner's Sons, 1947.

Wyllys, George. *The Wyllys Papers (1590-1796): Correspondence and Documents Chiefly of Descendants of Gov. George Wyllys of Connecticut*. Vol. 21, Collections of the Connecticut Historical Society. Hartford: Connecticut Historical Society, 1924.

Materials without a named author

"Clan Colquhoun." Electric Scotland, http://www.electricscotland.com/webclans/atoc/colquho.html.

"William Pynchon." In *Appleton's Cyclopedia of American Biography*, edited by James Grant Wilson, John Fiske and Stanley L. Klos. New York: D. Appleton and Company. Reprint, 1999.

"Winthrop Family Papers [Transcripts], 1630-1741." Boston: Massachusetts Historical Society.

The Civil Wars: A Military History of England, Scotland, and Ireland 1638-1660. Edited by John and Jane Ohlmeyer Kenyon. Oxford: Oxford University Press, 1998.

The Columbia Encyclopedia. New York: Columbia University Press, 2001.

The Literatures of Colonial America: An Anthology Edited by Susan P. Castillo and Ivy Schweitzer. Malden, MA: Blackwell Publishers, 2001.

"Another Springfield First! The First Book Banned in the New England Colonies Was Written by William Pynchon, Founder of Springfield, Massachusetts." Springfield City Library, http://www.springfieldlibrary.org/Pynchon/pynchon.html#pynchon.

Notes

Organized by chapter, each note references the text page and key words, which are usually the critical words glossed by the note. Publications cited—for example, (Chase 1919, 9:3)—are detailed in the Bibliography.

Prelude: A New World and a New Venture

1. **Thomas King**: While Winthrop had a companion on his journey, he is not named in his journal account. However, Thomas King is a likely choice, as he was a witness in 1644 to transactions with the Indians regarding the mine, and is thought to be a "prospective contractor, aiming to perform the first mining in this country"(Chase 1919, 9:3).

4. **a city of 1,500 souls**: an estimate from available figures: http://www.iboston.org/mcp.php?pid=popFig (accessed 2/15/09).

4. **The Winthrops did well**: The structure of a religious state made it such that the community leaders were involved in church *and* civic governance, and they were also well placed to benefit from expanding commerce. Winthrop's own home in Boston, for example, was merely a few blocks from the main port and from another harbor in which he had a substantial economic interest (see map, p. 23). The Puritans saw no contradiction in godliness and affluence.

5. **this snowy night in November, 1645**: The journey is described in detail by Winthrop himself, writing in Latin, which was translated in 1940 by William Carlton and published with his commentary in the *New England Quarterly* (Carlton 1940).

5. **another new Puritan settlement**: In later years the river would be known as Thames and the settlement, New London.

5. **black lead**: In fact, it was not lead but graphite.

6. **a surveying party the year before**: Black 1966, 125.

6. **silver was said to be mixed**: Ibid, 126.

6. **the Great River, which was frozen**: Carlton 1940, 501.

6. **the tiny colony's independently-minded governor**: William Pynchon was the founder and leading citizen of Springfield, a staunch Puritan but of an independent turn of mind. Only a few years later, that turn was to put him

at odds with accepted Puritan doctrine in Massachusetts, when a religious work that he wrote caused a furor. *The Meritorious Price of Our Redemption* was banned—the first book to be banned in Boston—and Pynchon was summoned before the Massachusetts magistrates and ordered to retract his statements. This was May 1651. Sometime in the following year, he had not yet recanted but instead transferred his property to his son, John, and then returned to England, never to return.

6. **the daughter of a governor of Connecticut:** Amy Wyllys' father, George, had been the governor of the Connecticut Colony in 1643. He had died in March 1645.

7. **your wedding last month:** although the Pynchon, Winthrop, and Wyllys families were all of the elites and certainly known to each other, it was unlikely that Winthrop would have been invited to or attended the wedding of John and Amy in October 1645. Weddings were not yet an occasion for gathering of families among the sober Puritans. In fact is it considered unlikely that Winthrop attended the wedding of even his own daughter, Elizabeth, in 1658 (Black 1966, 188).

8. **still living in Roxbury:** see "William Pynchon" in Appleton 1999.

8. **We are in need of iron tools:** Winthrop's rationale for iron is much as his father and he argued repeatedly and was widely accepted by the Puritan elites. For a detailed treatment of iron mining, see Innes 1995, 237-50.

9. **valuable exports of iron tools:** Black 1966, 112.

9. **"John Becx...bought forty":** Ibid, 117.

9. **The company were granted...exempt from all taxes:** Lewis 1844, 123.

10. **our rights to all vacant land:** This is the convenient doctrine of *vacuum domicilium*, promulgated by John Winthrop, Sr. (Trent 1982, 67).

11. **it continues for a few more lines:** " ... of Mystick, and do confirm the former sale of the Blacklead hill and the land about it at Tantiusques by Webuckshem until the said John Winthrop, and am fully satsfied for the same witness my hand this 11th Novr. 1644." This concludes the deed (Chase 1919, 9:3).

Chapter 1. Survivor

13. **the *John and Sara* :** The woman in the ship's name is sometimes spelled "Sarah" in references, but the spelling "Sara," written in the original letters of instruction from Becx and his partners to the ship's captain and to their agent in New England, is preferred here.

13. **that chill November morning**: November 11, 1651 is the date of the letter to Captain Greene (The New England Historical and Genealogical Society 1847: 377-380).

13. **not only Becx was involved**: Becx's two partners – or at least the two partners who signed the letter to the captain, if there were others – were "Rob't Rich" and "Will Greene" (in the transcribed copy of the recorder in New England). It's possible that Rich was either the second, or third, Earl of Warwick (father or son), both of whom were alive at this time and influential Puritans.

13. **Cromwell ordered that the prisoners of war be deported**: The "ordnance of Parliament" was dated October 21, 1651 (Ibid).

13. **the letter handed him by Becx**: Ibid.

13. **the fee that Mr. Kemble earns as each man is indentured**: Becx and his partners "consign(e)" the prisoners to Kemble, and though a fee or percentage is not specifically mentioned in the extant letter, given the nature of this transaction it was very unlikely to have been the first between the London undertakers and Kemble. Arrangements for a fee had likely been established previously. Text of the letter follows:

London, this 11: of Nouember 1651:

Mr. Tho: Kemble

Wee whose names are vnder written, freighters of the sh[ipp] John & Sara whereof is Commander John Greene Doe Consigne the said shipp & servants to be disposed of by yow for our best Advantage & account & whole proceed of the Servants & voyage Retourne in a jojnct stocke without any Division in such goods as you conceive will turne best to accont in the Barbadoes & consign them to Mr. Charles Rich for the aforesaid accott & wt other pay yow meete with fit for this place send hither & take the Advise and Assistance of Capt Jno Greene in disposall of the Servants Dispatch of the shipp or wt else may any wajes concern the voyage thus wishing the shipp a safe vojage & God's blessing on the same not doubting of your best care and dilligence, Remajne: your loving freinds Jo: Becx, Robt Rich, Willjam Greene.

Entered and Recorded at the Instant Request of the said Mr. Tho Kemble. Edw. Rawson Recorder 13th May 1652
(New England Historic Genealogical Society 1847).

14 . **the clan decided to throw in its lot with the king**: Two matters require elaboration regarding clan Colquhoun.

1. The clan name pronunciation is not at all obvious to contemporary Americans but is "sometimes pronounced Co'hoon" (http://www.loch-lomond.net/theloch/clans/colquhoun.html; accessed 2/23/08). Scottish surnames have an extraordinary number of related spellings and variants, as some of those related to Colquhoun indicate:
Colwhoun, Collquhone, Colchoun, Colhoune, Culchoun, Culquhoun, Culqwon, Culquhoune, Culwone, Culqwhone, Culqwone, Culquhone, Culchon, Culchone, Cowquhowne, Gahn, . . . Quohon, Qulwone, Maccoan, Maccowen, Maccowne, Mackowean, Mackownne, Mackowne, Mackowyne, Mackowen, Mackowie, Mackowin, Macowen, Macowan (http://www.electricscotland.com/webclans/atoc/colquho.html; accessed 2/23/08)

2. The evidence and reasoning for the clan's participation—and Daniel's—in the battle of Worcester includes:

a) As mentioned above, the clan surname leads to various related clan names, including, it seems likely, the John "Coehon," Senly [sic] "Mackonne," David "Mackhome," and our Dan: [sic] "Mackhoe" who were all recorded on board the *John and Sara*, and were thus all prisoners captured at the battle of Worcester. The likely semi-literate English soldiers who took down the names can be assumed to have had no love for the renegade and defeated Scots, and probably little opportunity to correct misspellings, if they had had the initiative and time, and if, indeed, the Scots were all literate or certain of the English spellings themselves and would have even noted errors. It seems most likely that the spellings are phonetic and what a scribe heard at one pass.

b) Support for the interpretation of clan Colquhoun members on board the ship is that the passenger recorded as John "Coehon" is changed (and presumably corrected) to "Colquhoun" on his arrival and listing in New England (New England Historic Genealogical Society 1847).

c) Dobson, in his dictionary of banished Scots, lists our Daniel Mackhoe (Daniel "Maccoe") as a "Royalist solder captured at Worcester. Transported from Gravesend to Boston on the *John and Sarah* "[sic] (Dobson, 1983, 238).

d) Mackenzie, in his compendium of family histories, asserts of Cone that "this family is of Scotch ancestry and is descended from Daniel MackHoe, who later was known as Daniel Cone" (Mackenzie, 1912, n.p.). Mackenzie further claims that Daniel was "an officer in the Scottish Army and was at the battle of Dunbar" [sic]. No primary references are known for Mackenzie.

e) The clan "seems almost certain to have been at the Battle of Worcester" according to research collected by an American authority on seventeenth century Scot immigrants (Diane Rapaport, e-mail to author, Jan. 26, 2006).

However, it does *not* seem likely that one of the known Scottish participants in the battle, the "Tolquhon Foot" soldiers, led by a Col. Walter Forbes, is a transcription error for "Colquhoun," as has been suggested. Col. Walter Forbes of Tolquhon, a locale near Aberdeen, Scotland, was a supporter of Charles II, and while it is not clear whether he or his eldest son, Alexander, were both present at the battle of Worcester, at least one very likely was (Anderson, 1862: 709).

16. **Daniel MacCoan**: Another possibility for Daniel's name is the spelling "Maccone," which is a name listed in the standard historical reference for Scottish surnames (Black, G., 1946: n.p.).

16. **The clerk, his uncertainty quickly mastered by indifference**: "While [the list] is fortunate for historical purposes, yet [it] is not to be accepted as a true record of their correct names" is the considered opinion of many who have studied the ship's list (Banks 1927, 19).

16. **the bread and cheese were often moldy, the beer sour**: Atkin 1998, 34.

17. **as the old general had been ill**: Ibid, 12.

17. **army of 10,000 Scots**: Ibid, 118.

17. **were short the weapons they needed**: Ibid, 30.

17. **lead musketball ripped through him**: graphic descriptions of war wounds are in Atkin 1998, 118.

18. **the cookfire was contained inside an open-top box**: Parthesius 2003.

18. **beans were soaking in the kettles**: a typical shipboard diet of the era is briefly covered in Schama 2007.

19. **the ministers ordered General Leslie**: the sorry mismanagement of Dunbar is presented well by Bell 1998.

20. **I ate only some peas**: the Scottish prisoners were treated detestably, at least by the enlightened standards of the modern Geneva conventions (Atkin 1998, 126).

20. **Durham, the cathedral there**: The Durham imprisonment sounds absolutely harrowing (Ibid).

Chapter 2. New England, Old Servitude

22. **He heard that some men had died**: Atkin 1998, 132.

22. **that February morning**: Although primary sources are not known, some researchers assert that the arrival was February 24, 1652 (Greubel 1997, 3). This would have been a winter voyage of about 14 weeks, somewhat more than the nine or ten weeks of the average duration, according to records kept by John Winthrop, Sr. For a discussion of the duration of Atlantic crossings, see Virginia DeJohn Anderson, *New England's Generation: The Great Migration and the Formation of Society. . .* Cambridge Univ. Press 1991, p. 71. The one date documented in a primary source relative to the arrival of the *John and Sara* is May 14, 1652, on which Edward Rawson recorded the ship's (undated) arrival "at the request of Mr. Thomas Kemble" (New England Historical and Genealogical Society, 1847: 379). However, it is very unlikely that the ship arrived in May, as that would have been a voyage of about seven months, which is longer than any documented between London and Boston. A February arrival seems much more likely.

23. **28 Scots had died**: Atkin 1998, 132.

24. **The Scots were marched**: Ibid. Boat transport from Boston to Lynn can't be completely ruled out, however.

24. **ferried across:** As the prisoners would have had to cross the Saugus to arrive in Lynn, it's entirely possible that Daniel crossed the river on the ferry which had formerly (1639-41) been operated by his future father-in-law, Gerard Spencer (Harold L. Spencer, Jr.. *A Spencer Genealogy: The Descent from Gerard of Haddam, Conn.* 1977, 19; cited in a Biographical sketch of Gerard Spencer, http://www.familyorigins.com/users/b/l/o/Peter-E-Blood/FAMO5-0001/d56.htm#P1316).

24. **Becx had paid**: Actually, Becx and his Undertaker partner, Joshua Foote (Carlson 2005, 2).

24. **For six or seven years more**: A contemporary source for this duration of servitude is the Rev. John Cotton who wrote Oliver Cromwell about the treatment of the Dunbar prisoners in Massachusetts Bay: "They have not been sold for slaves to perpetual servitude, but for 6 or 7 or 8 years. . . ."(Atkin 1998, 133). Note that Cotton's statement mixes the terms "slaves" and "servitude." See the next note.

24. **with very few rights**: Diane Rapaport, a lawyer who has researched and written about the prisoners, writes: "I've come to the conclusion that few of those Scottish war prisoners were sold/indentured/released with any formal papers or legal documentation. The only evidence of a formal indenture that I've come across, in all my research, was for a thirteen-year-old boy named

Alexander Gordon. Unlike the other Scots who came over on either the *Unity* [the year before] or the *John and Sarah*, Gordon was singled out for rescue at one of the London prison camps by a Massachusetts doctor, who brought Gordon back to America and then sold him to a Watertown, Mass. family. We only know of Gordon's indenture because he went to court in an effort to regain his freedom. But I've found absolutely no other evidence of indentures among the Scottish war prisoners, probably because the sales were all done informally, either through the Lynn ironworks, where most of the first shipload temporarily went first, or through the Charlestown, Mass. merchant who handled disposal of the second shipload of men. I no longer even refer to these Scots as 'indentured servants,' because I think they were a special case, more akin to short-term slavery or involuntary servitude (slavery was not necessarily assumed to be for life, or even race-based, in the mid 1600s, in New England, at least – the lines between slavery and servitude were blurred, until the last quarter of the seventeenth century) (Diane Rapaport, e-mail to author, Nov. 7, 2008).

24. **probably not Campbell**: Kemble would probably be spelled Kimball today.

24. **Kemble had connections to sawmills**: "This Thomas Kemble was part owner with Valentine Hill in the mills at Durham Falls and Lamprey River. He also owned lands in Maine and did an extensive business in lumber. He saw that the young Scotch prisoners would be useful men in sawmills and so he disposed of many of them in this way" (Stackpole 1913, 1: 75). The merchant, Valentine Hill, was also a business partner of the Bay's governor, John Winthrop, with whom in 1642 he undertook the development of the Boston's second commercial waterfront, at Shelter Cove (Whitehill 1968, 11). So the Winthrop family had at least some prior business ties to Thomas Kemble.

24. **the Undertakers of the Iron Mines had hired**: Dow 1895, 75.

25. **Leader apologized. . .was gone**: Ibid.

25. **Leader had taken twenty of them then**: Carlson 2005, 2.

25. **salt pork . . . porridge**: Black 1966, 57.

26. **I will choose twenty of you**: Stackpole 1913, 1: 76.

26. **Daniel quickly stepped forward in front of Leader**: While I have no documentary evidence that Daniel was indentured first to Leader, such an interpretation seems to me to best fit the available facts:

1) There is no direct evidence that Daniel is indentured to John Winthrop, Jr. (JW2) until 1657, and since JW2 himself was very unlikely to have been at Lynn in February 1652, it would depend on his having a known agent there,

if he were to have acquired Daniel then. Although Thomas Kemble seems possibile, there is no evidence of a direct relationship between him and JW2.

2) However, JW2 has been on good, indeed friendly terms with Richard Leader since his journey to England to raise funds for the Undertakers. As an expert in iron mining, Leader would have been a valuable advisor to JW2 and the other investors. JW2 maintained some contact with him after Leader replaced him as manager of the ironworks in 1645.

3) As of 1650 Leader was the manager of the Great Works sawmill operation in what is now Berwick, Maine, in which Becx was a primary owner. So Leader would almost certainly have been apprised of the Scots' conveyance to Boston, since Becx had acquired the Scots partly to furnish labor for his New England business interest (Rapaport 2004).

4) Documentary evidence cited by Rapaport shows that Leader in fact acquired about 20 Scots in both 1651 (the refugees from Dunbar) and 1652 (the refugees from Worcester). It's possible that Leader was not present at Lynn to indenture the Scots personally but instead worked through a trusted agent, most likely Kemble. However, that a relatively select pool of workers was obtained–1 of 10 available–argues for someone making the selection who was consequentially involved.

5) If Daniel was indentured first to Leader and proved himself worthy, the skills of logging and charcoal making, which he would have likely learned with Leader, would have been desirable to JW2, and we know that Daniel is involved in these labors for JW2.

6) As to how Daniel passes to JW2, transfer of indenture was not uncommon, and we know of at least one other transfer in which JW2 was involved (see note to p. 29 re: Henry Salmon). The friendly relations between Leader and JW2 would have provided the opportunity. JW2's need for assistance in both charcoal-making and mining when he went to New Haven in 1656 would have recommended Daniel to him by then.

26. **Body of Liberties**: this section on slavery is particularly indebted to Jordan 1971. The cited document dates from 1641.

26. **Bond-slavery**: Jordan 1971, 31. As with quoted material on slavery in notes following, the full quote here has been shortened, but the original sense is retained.

26. **but for 6 or 7 or 8 years**: See note to p. 24, citing Rapaport.

26. **your bondsmen forever**: According to Jordan, Leviticus 25:45, 46 is the source.

27. **20 Moores cheaper**: Jordan 1971, 33.

27. **African slave**: Ibid, 32.

27. **a particularly well-to-do group**: Osterweis 1953, 8.

27. **making himself the wealthiest in the colony:** Osterweis 1953, 22-23.

27. **the Sabbath prohibitions on cooking, bedmaking**: Black 1966, 176.

28. **mostly finished with 10 years ago**: All the sordid details of Nicholas and Ester Pinions' married life and JW2's relationship with Nicholas is examined in Innes 1995, 261-3.

28. **But the man could be reformed**: "New England authorities. . . displayed surprising confidence that the culture of discipline eventually would bring such types [Pinion] to heel"(Innes 1995, 263).

28. **Wee must delight in eache other**: John Winthrop, *A Modell of Christian Charity* (1630) in Miller and Johnson 1938, 198.

28. **hard to leave what he had built:** Black 1966, 174.

28. **he remembered the friendly overtures**: Ibid, 177.

29. **His father had said that iron**: Innes 1995, 244.

29. **He had borrowed a saddle from Leader**: Dow 1895, 75.

29. **over two decades' time**: Winthrop acquired servants as early as 1635, with the Saybrook enterprise (Games 1999, 78, 80).

29. **that fellow, Salmon, whom he had let go two years before**: The transactions of the indenture of Henry Salmon (variously Sawman, Sawmon, Sammon, and Samon) are detailed in several successive manuscript pages in the *Winthrop Family Papers* collection of the Massachusetts Historical Society. The documents begin with the June 17, 1653 transfer of Salmon's indenture to John Chester from Chester's mother. Salmon then passes to Robert Griffin, who assigns his rights in Salmon to John Winthrop, Jr., of Pequid (Pequot/New London) on February 14, 1654; and Winthrop "resigns all my rights in Henry Salmon unto John Elderkin," for "one whole year" on April 14, 1655. Whether Salmon's passage to Elderkin was his last, why he was such hot property, and if this number of masters (5) during this period was at all typical are not known (much of this history is also in vol. 6 of *Winthrop Papers*, Massachusetts Historical Society 1992).

32. **He made one broad stroke**: The contents of the agreement between Cotter and Winthrop, witnessed by Cone (appears to be spelled "Conn") and Davis, and the manner of the handwriting of all are drawn directly from a manuscript viewed (and photocopied from microfilm): *Winthrop Papers*, Agreement of William Cotter with John Winthrop, Jr., May 11, 1657, MHS.

35. **they had the ground cleared**: A detailed seventeenth century English account of charcoaling for ironworks is in Evelyn 1908, 113-117.

37. **in comparison to his own sons:** "But his children . . . can not have always been a satisfaction" summarizes a detailed story of sons Fitz and Wait contained in Black's admirable biography, *The Younger John Winthrop* (Black 1966).

38. **of how things truly are:** this conversation and charge to Daniel to observe the mining operations are constructed from a string of facts and inferences:

1) The agreement with Cotter is signed May 11, 1657, in New Haven (see note to p. 32 above).

2) On May 21, 1657 the General Court in Hartford had elected Winthrop the governor of the Connecticut Colony, and he would have received notice of this some time later and made a plan to visit Hartford to discuss the appointment, perhaps by mid-June, 1657.

3) Meanwhile, the Tantiusques operation had resumed or was resuming, as is known from the account books of John Pynchon; Winthrop would have wanted to assess its costs and benefits to him, as he was now contemplating a period of transition—the move from New Haven to Hartford—and presumably an increasing obligation on his time for public, not private, matters, as governor.

4) Daniel is named on a receipt for goods received from John Pynchon, and since the receipt also names William Deines, the overseer of the Tantiusques mine, likely Daniel was at the mine, and working there, before receiving the Pynchon receipt. Although it is undated, the transaction likely occurred in the second half of 1657, and before the onset of winter weather, when mining activities would have been suspended. In any case, Winthrop's move to Hartford appears to have been complete by December 1657, as then he is documented as first in office as governor. (For more on this transaction see the next chapter and notes there.)

5) At some point before March 1658 Daniel has been one of two guarantors of a loan made to a James Parker by Richard Fellows. *How would Daniel have considered himself able to back the loan?*

As Daniel splits the guarantee of the £15 (pound) loan with another man, John Cockrill, Daniel would have had to feel comfortable about guaranteeing probably half that amount. Seven pounds is a great deal of money, as 15 pounds is regarded as being a typical year's pay for an English day laborer (Innes 1995, 256). However, colliering was a well-compensated activity, and a collier could earn the same amount in a single month. It is possible that Daniel is paid some amount by Cotter for his labor (there is no stipulation in the agreement that Daniel and John Davis are *not* to be paid). Cotter owes

Winthrop £10 to be paid in charcoal; presumably this weight would have been the yield of one good firing. At that point, Cotter would have had an established relationship with Daniel, and could certainly have continued to employ him. Under standard indentured agreements, the servant could work a certain number of days of the week (often three days) to earn income for himself. So, even if Daniel had no other source of funds to back the Parker loan, colliering after May 1657 could have provided it.

38. **as hard dispute as ever he met with**: letter from Emmanuel Downing to John Winthrop, Jr., Jan. 7, 1652 (Massachusetts Historical Society 1992, 184).

39. **at the Winthrop home**: Ibid, 383.

Chapter 3. The Governor's Trust

40. **Daniel followed the road north from Hartford**: This chapter's narrative is constructed from the very few primary source documents available:

 1) John Pynchon's account book entry naming Daniel (see note to p. 45 below)

 2) John Winthrop, Jr.'s decision, by early 1658, to reduce his involvement with the Tantiusques mine, at least in part because of what today we might call an unfavorable cost/benefit ratio (to be more fully presented in the next chapter)

 3) Winthrop's letter to Stuyvesant on Daniel's behalf requires the plausible circumstances in which Daniel and John Cockrill would have become known to each other in a context in which they would then guarantee James Parker's loan to Richard Fellows. This must have occurred sufficiently before March 1658 such that Fellows knew of the flight of Cockrill and Parker to New Amsterdam and was satisfied they would not be paying him, which occasioned his demand of Daniel for payment, no doubt Daniel's dismay at this (also to be treated in Chapter 4).

40. **William Pynchon . . . successful merchant**: Smith 1961, 12ff.

41. **Mr. Winthrop's man**: This sense of "man," meaning servant, was in use at the time; the *Oxford English Dictionary* definition #10 for "man" cites a 1639 passage from New England with this meaning.

42. **Cabooder**: Waters 1899, 70.

43. **how a man goes about it can make a great difference**: A thoughtful account of the profound shift in values from nature to artifact, land to

commerce, that was occurring in the mid-seventeenth century is chapter 5, "Feudalism vs. Capitalism" in Talpalar 1976.

43. **Ashquoash**: Carlton 1940, 500.

43. **a large pond**: today known as Leadmine Pond.

44. **vein of minerals**: "The cut along the top of the ridge is the partially filled-in remainder of what was once a several thousand foot-long trench, 20 to 50 feet in depth and roughly 6 feet in width, that followed the vein of graphite" (Trustees 2005, n.p.).

44. **working off indenture**: Exact figures for the Bay Colony or Connecticut at this time are unknown. But since the 1630s, economic and social dislocation, separate from religious beliefs, had driven many thousands from the British Isles to become servants in the colonies. In the mid-1630s approximately one-third of New Englanders were indentured servants (Games 1999, 74).

45. **a one pound credit for his labor**: It seems reasonable to assume a rate of £1 per week, since two month's mine labor at Tantiusques in August 1658 was paid £8 (Pynchon 1985, 255).

45. **Kersey and Peniston woolens**: Kersey was "coarse, narrow cloth woven from long wool, and usually ribbed"; Peniston was "coarse Yorkshire woolen cloth used for garments or lining" (list of cloth terms: Pynchon 1985, xxiii).

45. **Pynchon wrote in his account book**: the account book ledger is copied exactly here (Pynchon 1985, 273).

46. **a man some years older**: the birth year of Richard Fellows appears unknown, but as he was a "freeman" in Hartford in 1645 (Morris 1940) this suggests that he was at least 21 at that time and a property owner of some significance (Fowler 1958, 315n).

47. **take my note**: The Mass. Hist. Society has a record that Richard was in Boston March 9, 1658, having letters from JW2 to business associates. In 1658 Richard Fellows was proposed as contractor for moving ore from lead mines in Springfield, and he removed his family from Hartford to Springfield about this same year. A record of the Mass. Bay Colony shows that he certified to having laid out 300 acres in the Connecticut River valley for a Boston investor.

47. **servant Edmond**: In June 1657 a letter from Jonathan Brewster in New London to Winthrop refers to "your servant Edmond, with his wife, now at my house, desyred me to informe your Worshipp that they ar all well upon the Iland" (Waters 1899, 51).

47. **when Daniel joined Mr. Winthrop's service in 1656**: This date is two years prior to the letter of Winthrop to Peter Stuyvesant, which is routinely

cited as the earliest document identifying Daniel Cone. Cone is identified in the bill of a merchant, Theodore Atkinson, to Mr. John Winthrop "of Peaquit, debter too Theoder Atkinson. The bill lists "Item: A Cutt Fealt [hat] to Daniell Cone" for 15 shillings, incurred "9:7:56," i.e., July 9, 1656 (Bill of Theodore Atkinson, Sept. 3, 1658 (?), Winthrop Papers (corrected typescript copy), Mass. Historical Soc.) In 1656, Winthrop and presumably Daniel were residing in Pequit (Pequot/New London).

47. **share his bed with another man:** A brief account of living conditions at the "Scotts House" is Atkin 1998, 132. However, ironworks records suggest that many of the Scots were "leased" to other ironworkers, with whom they boarded (D. Rapaport, e-mail to author, Sept. 11, 2009).

47. **ironworks had not done well:** the Undertakers management of Hammersmith went into bankruptcy by October 1657, but the exact date, and more to the point here, the exact consequences to the Scot laborers at the time, are not certain (Innes 1995, 268).

48. **this mill was one of only a very few:** Hartley 1957, 176-77.

49. **making the interior only hotter:** a good summary of Hammersmith is National Park Service, Saugus Iron Works--Reading 2, National Park Service, http://www.cr.nps.gov/nr/twhp/wwwlps/lessons/30saugus/30facts2.htm.

52. **much easier to crack open:** In a long letter from John Winthrop, Jr., then in Boston, to his son in England, Sept. 12, 1658, JW2 says: "There is some black-lead digged, but not so much as they expected it being very difficult to get out of the rocks, wch they are forced to break with fires, the rocks being very hard and not to be entered farther than the fire maketh way, so as yecharge hath been so greate in digging of it that I am like to have no profit by ye same" (Chase 1919, 10:3).

Chapter 4. Judgment

54. **"I shall be sorry to leave New Haven":** Black 1966, 179.

54. **"Mr. Paine and Mr. Clark will market":** Winthrop made arrangements Sept. 25, 1657 with William Paine and Thomas Clark, merchants of Boston, for the disposal of the product in the market. The merchants also advanced a sum to finance the business.

55. **they would only lease it:** Black 1966, 179.

55. **exchanged lengthy and acrimonious letters:** Hooker 1860 presents the letters in full, and some interpretation is offered by Andrews 1934, 25.

55. **Hooker had been dead for ten years:** Hooker died July 7, 1647.

55. **Winthrop that founded the Saybrook colony**: Black 1966, 88.

55. **re-elected to that role every two years**: successive tenures were not permitted.

55. **Winthrop did not participate**: Black 1966, 177.

55. **invited him again in August**: Trumbull 1850, 301. And again, it's worth noting that a governor of a New England colony at this time is more like a chairman of the board of a corporation than like a publicly elected state governor of modern times (Black 1966, 43).

55. **the negro Cabooder**: Cabooder (a.k.a. "Strange" and "Caboonder") is mentioned in a July 1661 last will of JW2, as "his negro" (Waters 1899, 70).

56. **Reverend Davenport as he continued his sermon**: This sermon, actually given after Davenport had moved from New Haven to Boston, is one of the few extant by him, and probably represents his characteristic themes and language. John Davenport, *Gods Call to His People to Turn Unto Him; Together with His Promise to Turn Unto Them*, Early American Imprints. 1st Series; No. 137. (Cambridge [Mass.]: Printed by S.G. [Samuel Green] and M.J. [Marmaduke Johnson] for John Usher of Boston, 1669).

57. **Could be sold for a debt**: See Jernagan, 1971.

57. **total depravity of men:** This notion of total depravity is one of the five principal beliefs of Calvinism, which Davenport would have subscribed to. See Bowden, http://mb-soft.com/believe/txc/puritani.htm.

57. **houses were built**: Love 1914, 155.

58. **by the grateful colonists at their own expense**: Black 1966, 179.

58. **John Winthrop's five girls**: Ibid, 180.

58. **all of his girls had fallen ill with the measles**: Ibid.

60. **pay for winter clothing for his older sister and her two young children:** This is a plausible calamity at this period, but there is no documentary evidence of Parker's sister. In fact, other than the naming of Cockrill and Parker in the letter from Winthrop to Stuyvesant (see note to p. 65), no other information is know about them (John Winthrop, Jr., to Peter Stuyvesant, March 2, 1658, *Winthrop Family Papers*, Mass. Historical Soc., editor's annotations.)

60. **guaranteeing the loan to Parker**: This reconstruction of events is inferred from existing evidence and the letter to Stuyvesant (see note next page).

60. **For twice that much in personal property**: Taylor 1979, 23.

62. **a summons that came to every able-bodied man**: Taylor 1979, 16.

63. **half-way covenant ... too liberal**: A detailed religious history of early Connecticut notes:

"The Half-Way Covenant was presented to the Connecticut General Court, August, 1657. Orders were at once given that copies of it should be distributed to all the churches with a request for a statement of any exceptions that any of them might have to it. None are known to have been returned. This was not due to any great unanimity of sentiment among the churches, for in Connecticut, as elsewhere, many of the older church-members were not so liberally inclined as their ministers, and were loth to follow their lead in this new departure" (Greene 1905, n.p.).

64. **I am no stranger to court**: Court records indicate Fellows was a litigious individual. Later, in March 1662, he was plaintiff in two lawsuits in Hampton County court: one against a man for taking some bricks from him, and another against a woman for defaming him (Smith 1961, 259).

64. **no such request has been made before**: It is asserted by the principal early twentieth century genealogist of the Cone family that this was "one of the first" instances in North America of an extradition request between two leaders of government (Cone 1903, 11).

65. **Much honored Sir**: I have updated antique and irregular spellings (e.g., "equal" instead of "equall") and also made the spelling of the given names consistent with modern versions (e.g., "Daniel" instead of "Daniell"). (John Winthrop, Jr., to Peter Stuyvesant, March 2, 1658, Winthrop Papers (corrected typescript copy), Mass. Historical Soc.)

65. **the name, Peter Stuyvesant**: Unfortunately, we may never know the resolution of this matter, or at least the reply, if any, from Stuyvesant, unless it be found among as yet unidentified papers of John Winthrop, Jr. A detailed account of Stuyvesant's correspondence in 1658 indicates that no letter to other than Dutch officials would be found, as other outgoing correspondence would have been copied to "letter books," none of which have survived (Gehring and Stuyvesant 2003. p. xix).

67. **the native would confirm Winthrop's ownership rights**: In fact, on March 1, William Deines witnessed the confirmation of the deed of 1644 (Chase 1919, 10:6).

67. **Gardiner was three decades his senior**: Gardiner was born in 1599, Arthur Howell in 1632.

68. "**... PINS!**":Elizabeth Gardiner's quoted statements are as presented in depositions made after her death in Easthampton (Demos 1982, 213 footnote).

69. **Gardiner received the commission**: Tomlinson 1978, 1.

69. **one was captured and roasted alive**: Ibid, 3.

69. **he himself had retreated to Boston**: Lion Gardiner noted this departure in his account of the Pequot War, written in 1660 (and thus after the 1658 trial of Goody Garlick): " . . . for they [Winthrop and others] said they would have their [Pequot] lives and not their presents; then I answered, Seeing you will take Mr. Winthrop to the Bay to see his wife, newly brought to bed of her first child, and though you say he shall return, yet I know if you make war with these Pequits, he will not come hither again, for I know you will keep yourselves safe, as you think, in the Bay, but myself, with these few, you will leave at the stake to be roasted, or for hunger to be starved. . ." (Gardiner 1860, 9).

70. **the couple had worked for him**: The relationship between the Garlicks and Gardiners and the rest of the townspeople is discussed in compelling detail in Demos, pp. 213-241.

71. **delivering the governor's messages**: Although no documentary evidence has been found identifying Daniel in this role as the governor's messenger, Daniel is almost certainly indentured at this time, and the role seems very plausible, given the governor's manifest consideration of him and the need for this function. Certainly the governor himself would be unlikely to carry official messages on a routine basis.

71. **Several years older**: approximately five years, as Daniel was said to be 80 at his death in 1706, thus born in 1626. Samuel as born in 1631 (Wyllys 1924, xxxvi).

71. **an oak tree and its large trunk**: Some years later this becomes the famous "charter oak," in which Connecticut's charter is hidden from agents of the King.

71. **Ruth. . . the baby**: Samuel married Ruth Haynes, the daughter of the recent governor, in 1654; their first child, Mary, was born in 1656.

71. **Indictment**: an accessible copy, http://covenantofrhiannon.org/garlick.htm (accessed 7/28/2009)

72. **the last one in Wethersfield**: John and Joan Carrington were tried, convicted, and executed in 1651.

72. **"If any man or woman . . . "**: Tomlinson 1978, 3.

72. **mark in the woman's most private**: for a discussion of the marks of witches and the examination procedures to find them, see Demos 1982, 179-80.

72. **the inn on Main Street**: Love 1914, 216.

72. **the gentlemen magistrates**: Black (1966) identifies the listed group of magistrates; Tomlinson (1978) adds John Cullick and Henry Clark.

73. **he watched them fall into silence**: Winthrop's relationship with Gardiner runs deep. Apart from their dispute over the handling of the Pequots, they were both connected to the prominent Puritan theologian Hugh Peter. Through the Reverend Peter's connections, Gardiner had gotten the Saybrook commission. Peter was also John Winthrop, Jr.'s father-in-law.

73. **Matthew Allyn and Nathaniel Ward**: "The jury consisted of Matthew Allen [sic], David Wilton, Nathaniel Ward, Andrew Bacon, Edward Stebbing, William Wadsworth, Samuel Smith, Thomas Coleman, Nathaniel Dickerson, John Moore, John Strong, and Jasper Gunn" (Tomlinson 1978, 23).

74. **"Goodwife Birdsell testified**: Court deposition taken in Easthampton (Demos 1982, 218).

75. **Perhaps she was Dutch, or French:** Mary was in fact Dutch.

75. **'I am bewitched'**: As previously, all the direct quotes of the bedroom conversation as well as the history of relationship between the Gardiners and Garlicks comes from the invaluable reconstruction in Demos (1982, chapter 7 passim).

76. **"Gentle and loving friends"**: Winthrop's speech here is very similar to the letter from the court to the town and certainly approved by him (Demos 1982, 220).

76. **"We know that the majority of you"**: This "majority" observation is not in the official letter, but revealed by town records (Demos 1982, 219).

Chapter 5. Enduring Choices

77. **On Wednesday**: Proclamation decided at court, Aug. 23, 1658 (Trumbull 1850, 323).

78. **The weather had been wrong**: Black 1966, 182.

78. **the decline of virtuous behavior**: Just how concerned the Puritans were in this decline is a subject of Bozeman's *To Live Ancient Lives*: the Puritans' flight [to the colonies was] "to a free world in which long-lost biblical rules and ways could be reinstituted."

78. **he might not prevail**: Indeed, the United Colonies split the land involved in the disputes at this time (Black 1966, 183-84).

78. **such excesses as wine**: Black 1966, 187.

79. **"For the cariage of the lead". . . offering to lease**: On Oct. 12, 1658, Winthrop entered with Messrs. Paine and Clark into a fourteen-year lease of the lead mines and all other minerals that may be found; Winthrop was to

have "one third of the cleane product free of all charges." On November 16, 1658, William Deines, "servant to Mr. Payne in Boston in name and behalf of Mr. Winthrop" again obtained a deed for the site from "Wascomo, sachem of Tantiasquessek son of Webuckshams" (Chase 1919, 10: 3).

79. **A third of whatever their profits**: "I find in an account book of John Pynchon of Springfield, that Mr. William Paine and Capt. Thomas Clarke of Boston employed men to work at the black lead mine in 1657, 1658 and 1659, and perhaps some years later; and that Mr. Pynchon procured provisions for them, and paid the workmen considerable amount from his shop of goods. Mr. Winthrop is noticed two or three times as giving orders, but all the charges are made against Paine and Clarke, and they paid Pynchon's bill in goods, at Boston. The name of the principal workman, or overseer, was William Deins. Pork, bacon, Pease, bread flour, Indian meal, cheese &c were conveyed from Springfield to the mine on horseback. Pynchon's agency ceased in 1659, but the work may have been carried on some years longer, or until 1663" (Ibid).

79. **"There is some black-lead digged"**: letter to Fitz, Sept. 12, 1658 (Ibid).

80. **her eldest children**: John born 1636; Mehitable born 1638 (also see note p. 81 below).

80. **Gerard** [Spencer]: His name is variously spelled, including Jared and Jarred in Connecticut Colony court records, and Garrard in his own will (but Gerard in his uncle's will). As with most seventeenth century spellings, Gerard is likely just one phonetic equivalent, but the existence of the last "r" in his own will-variant suggests the sound was probably *not* like Jared—leaving Gerard a reasonable default spelling (Spencer 1907, 20).

80. **leave the town**: Those 30 members of the church represent only part of the presumed departures, as other family members and church-goers not officially recognized as members would also have departed (*First Church* 1885, 14).

80. **a community more to their liking**: Those 30 men—head of households who are "members" of the First Church of Hartford—signed an agreement April 18, 1659, to depart Hartford. They settled in Hadley; enough were there by November to call a town meeting. Richard Fellows was among first settlers (Walker 1906, 4).

80. **removal from Cambridge and Lynn**: a "great turmoil" occurred at Cambridge in the mid 1630s during which nearly all of the population removed to Hartford under Rev. Thomas Hooker and sold their property to followers of Rev. Thomas Shepard.

81. **eleven children**: after John and Mehitable (see note to p. 80) followed Hannah (1640), Marah (1642), Sarah (1644), Elizabeth (1646), Thomas (1648), Samuel (1650), Timothy (1652), Ruth (1654), William (1656), and Nathaniel (1658).

81. **in their twenties**: Although some sources put Mehitable's birth at 1642, the much more likely date is 1638, particularly if one believes the chronology of other children, including the birth of Mara in 1642.

81. **truly together, Hannah**: Love was more than an accident, it was a duty for married couples: "This duty of love is mutual, it should be performed by each, to each of them. They should endeavour to have their affections really, cordially, and closely knit, to each other" (Morgan 1956, p. 12 - quoting Benjamin Wadsworth, *The Well-ordered Family*).

81. **Thomas**: The earliest documentation for Thomas puts him in the Colonies by the end of 1633, apparently arriving as an unmarried man. He first settled in Cambridge and moved by 1636 to Hartford. This would place him among the earliest of Hartford settlers. He was referred to in his estate papers as "Sergeant" Thomas Spencer. He married Anne Dorryfall in 1634 and had three children by her. She died by 1645, and he then married Sarah Bearding in 1645 by whom he had six more children. He died at the age of 80 on Sept. 11, 1687, in Hartford. A furniture maker, he left his son, Jared, his shop and tools (Taylor 1998).

82. **martyr of the people**: *The Trials of Charles* 1861, 109.

83. **no disturbance in the world**: Ibid, 111.

83. **restored to the throne**: Charles II was restored in May 1660.

83. **shot from under him**: Ibid, 245.

83. **commanded a regiment**: Wikipedia entry on William Goffe (accessed 12/13/08).

84. **his clothes**: Daniel's clothing is that of a workman on a workday (Johnson 2002, 90).

86. **to attack the Pequots:** The standard reference for the attack on the Pequot village at Mystic (Orr 1897) collects three accounts by the lead English combatants and one other; these accounts influenced centuries of writers as different as the contemporary Puritan minister Thomas Shepard (Shepard 2001) and a modern writer for younger readers (Aronson 2004). However, the received accounts of the battle, all by English colonial participants, have been strenuously challenged by two independent historians who closely examined the historic accounts and found them wanting in light of their story contradictions, the physical circumstances of the alleged battle, and their ignorance of Indian culture and warfare. Wagner

and Dempsey bring an Indian perspective and sympathy to their reconstruction of events, and *Mystic Fiasco: How the Indians Won the Pequot War* (2003) raises a strong argument for itself. However, it concedes that Indians *were* killed at the village and the village *was* burned.

87. **We killed many Pequots**; Sources differ as to the number of Pequots killed, but the standard range is (remarkably) from 300 to 700—which suggests to Wagner and Dempsey (2003) that no body count is reliable; they suggest it may have been about 50 (p. 117). They argue, unlike the English combatants, that no women or children were killed. No forensic evidence appears to exist today.

87. **made me a sergeant of the militia**: Taylor 1998.

87. **a signer of the Magna Carta**: this assertion is considered in passing in Spencer 1997.

89. **they're from the king**: the visit of the king's officers, Thomas Kirke and Thomas Kellond, occurred May 10, 1661 (Black 1966, 203).

90. **their errand for the king**: Kirke and Kellond were searching for the regicides Whalley and Goffe.

92. **the Geneva Bible**: This classic, originally published in 1560, *not* the King James version, was the Bible of the Puritans.

92. **I came to the colonies**: Exactly when Gerard arrived is not certain, although some researchers assert that he arrived in Boston with Gov. Winthrop, Sr., in 1630 (Blood 2002). First documentary record puts Gerard in Cambridge in 1634 (Savage 1977, IV: 147). He was born in 1614, so regardless, Gerard would have been less than 20 years old on arrival.

93. **One man in every ten**: As the best scholarly study makes clear, accurate statistics about the incidence of syphilis in Elizabethan and Jacobean England are impossible to make, but the ratio of one in ten is safely within the range of best-documented examples available (Fabricius 1994, 30).

93. **their noses rotting away**: Fabricius 1994, 27.

93. **I should have taken offense**: In Elizabethan England, accusing a person of being syphilitic was considered defamation and slander, and subject to legal challenge (Fabricius 1994, 269).

94. **swear by this holy Bible**: ". . . the microbes of the Renaissance had repercussions also in the field of religion and morals, where theologians such as Martin Luther and John Calvin steered the development of Protestant ethics in the direction of sexual puritanism" (Fabricius 1994, 17). Fabricius documents the increasing focus of Puritans in the latter 16th and early 17th centuries on the scourge of syphilis and a kind of moral hysteria for cleanliness: It being "the duty of young men also to keep their bodies

unpolluted, undefiled, unspotted, free and utterly estranged from all whoredom and uncleaness," as one Puritan minister expressed it (Ibid, 111).

94. **discuss the marriage contract**: The marriage arrangement between Daniel and Mehitable may seem atypical, in that marriages were usually among social equals. Daniel very likely married by April 1662, as a first child, Ruth, was born Jan. 7, 1663. Hannah was born April 1664, reportedly in Haddam (Cone 1903, 13).

94. **Connecticut had no certain legal status**: Andrews 1934, 68.

95. **Thirty Mile Island**: so-called because the colonists believed that to be the distance from the river's mouth. It is considerably less, about 17 miles.

95. **Winthrop's departure for England in July 1661**: The royal patent was obtained by JW2 and received in Connecticut September 1662. JW2 returned to Connecticut June 1663.

95. **purchase from the local Indians**: Black, 179.

95. **Know all men**: Wyllys 1924, 137.

95. **Wyllys had received, on behalf of the colony . . . six miles into the country**: Parker 1938, n. p.: "The Settlement West Side of the Great River."

96. **Nine, as it happens**: Gerard bought nine parcels of land in Hartford ranging in size from 1.5 to 30 acres (Spencer 1997, 222).

Afterward: Proprietor, Freeman, Father

98. **vital statistics that are readily available**: The birth/baptismal dates are those cited in the standard genealogical source (Cone 1903, 12).

98. **by some accounts in Haddam**: Haddam birthplace according to W. W. Cone (op. cit.), but see note following

98. **Ebenezer baptized**: "christened" in some accounts.

98. **Elizabeth Cunningham**: W. W. Cone cites two wives, a first Elizabeth (no maiden name), and this second Elizabeth Cunningham (Cone 1903, 12).

98. **daughter Hannah**: The actual date of the marriage is not recorded, although it was "apparently" in 1665 (Parker 1938, 3).

99. **Gerard's relations were among the less well-off**: Parker 1938, 6.

99. **wheat valued at . . . 3.5 shillings**: This is the value JW2 placed on wheat he would supply in New London to meet a debt incurred in England in 1662, and thus seems like a reasonable standard of valuation for that time (Black 1966, 225).

99. **tradition** [re: settlement]: "Soon after this purchase" of Thirty Mile Island (Bayles 1884, 369).

99. **"immediately after the royal charter was issued"**: Cunningham and Warner 1994, 5.

99. **Haddam probably not settled until spring 1665**: Substantial circumstantial evidence is offered by Francis Parker to support his detailed argument for that date (Parker 1938, 3).

100. **Thomas. . . more likely than father-in-law Gerard**: Moreover, Gerard's livelihood in this period, other than as farmer and land-holder, is not known.

100. **the ceremonial chair**: This chair, most often attributed to the Spencer workshop (Trent 1984, 192), has also received a detailed analysis that argues against the Spencer origins (Kamil 2005, 247ff).

100. **On his return home**: JW2 arrived in Hartford, June 1663.

100. **Varlet, who was Dutch**: Capt. Nicholas Varlet, an officer in the Dutch W.I. Company, was a brother-in-law of Gov. Peter Stuyvesant (Trumbull 1850, 387n.).

100. **Mrs. Skreech. . . may have been Dutch, as well**: However, an English woman is a possible match, referenced in UK National Archives: http://www.nationalarchives.gov.uk/A2A/records.aspx?cat=027-3250a&cid=-1&Gsm=2008-06-18#-1

100. **Daniel knew Mrs. Skreech well enough to borrow from her**: Intriguing that the lender was a *Mrs.* Skreech – not a Mr. Skreech, suggesting that a husband was no longer living. . . .

100. **same court docket**: For information about this case, I am indebted to author Diane Rapaport (Rapaport, e-mail to author, Jan. 28, 2006):
At Quarter Court in Hartford, March 5, 1663:
"Mrs Mary Skreech pltf as Attourney to C: Nicholas Varlet Administratr ec contr Danll Cone Dfnt in an action of debt wth damadge 2 ll 18 s o d
Mrs Mary Skreech Pltf ec contr Peter Grant in an action of debt wth dam: 2 ll 12 s o d
Mary Skreech Pltf contr Peter Grant in an action of debt and damadge 1 ll 14 s o d"
Records of the Particular Court of Connecticut, 1639-1663 (1928, facsimile reprint, Bowie, Md.: Heritage Books, 1987), 265.

100. **Peter Grant**: Peter Grant was among the group of Scotch prisoners deported after Dunbar and put to work at the Great Works (Pirsig, 2008, 2).

100. **at the Saugus Ironworks**: ". . . maybe the Grant who started at the Massachusetts ironworks and ended up in Hartford?" (Rapaport, e-mail to author, Jan. 28, 2006)

100. **such a relationship supports**: although certainly does not prove.

100. **the verdict against Daniel**: Colonial Connecticut Records (CCR) website, CCR Volume 01, p 434:
www.colonialct.uconn.edu/NewCTScanImages/0015THEP/V0001/1000/04560434.jpg

101. **Capt. Richard Lord**: He was elected captain of the local troops under Major John Mason in March 1658.

101. **Lord. . . a resident of Hartford**: Although Capt. Richard Lord also had an "ambiguous grant" to some lands in the vicinity of Thirty Mile Island (Parker 1938, 3).

102. **at least seven of them**: Clarke, Gates, Smith, Corbee, Brainerd, Wells (but not Cone) (Parker 1938, 6).

102. **the burden . . . rested upon themselves**: Parker 1938, 6.

102. **Daniel's lot . . . edge of the settlement**: Why all the relatives did not take adjoining lots–except for Daniel and his brother-in-law–is not known. Perhaps they didn't want to; perhaps other circumstances (prior purchase) or considerations (desirable location) made it not possible.

103. **Salmon, abundant in those days**: "The salmon were so common in the river dividing East-Haddam from Haddam Neck, that it was called Salmon River from that circumstance" (Field 1814, 9).

103. **settlers . . . catch them in quantity**: Cunningham and Warner 1984, 6.

103. **the plantation, now called Haddam**: The name was selected by the town in 1668, "probably from Haddam or Hadham in England" (Field 1814, 6). Other sources explain the choice of name as associated with the first governor of the Colony, John Haynes, who supposedly "still had family connections" in Great Hadham, in Hertfordshire (Deming 1933, 37).

103. **"presented for freemen"**: Colonial Connecticut Records (CCR) website (http://www.colonialct.uconn.edu), CCR_Volime 02, p. 110.

104. **honest conversation**: A requirement as of 1657 (Taylor 1979, 23).

104. **The status of freeman was not exactly rare**: " . . . the extent of the franchise in the 1660's was broad. Probably most Connecticut men who were not servants could vote as freemen if they wanted to, except those men who, although otherwise qualified, had been unable to appear before the General Assembly or traveling magistrates to take the oath" (Fowler 1958, 333).

104. **Daniel was a commissioner**: Cone 1903, 12.

104. **"become one of the most important men in the new town"**: Parker 1938, 8.

104. **holding town offices**: "minor offices" (Cone 1903, 12).

104. **As late as 1703, colony court records list him**: Connecticut (Colony) 1850 vol 4: 429.

105. **our common enemy**: Cunningham and Warner 1984, 4.

105. **Gerard .. an ensign in Haddam militia**: See http:// www.familyorigins.com/users/b/l/o/Peter-E-Blood/FAM05-0001/ d56.htm#P1316. For lists of combatants, the standard reference is George M. Bodge's 1906 *Soldiers in King Philip's War* (available complete online).

105. **were never a substantial threat again**: See http://en.wikipedia.org/ wiki/King_Philip%27s_War

105. [Gerard Spencer] **last will**: (Manwaring 1995)

105. [Daniel's East Haddam] **dwelling house**: Parker 1938, 4.

105. **one historic account**: Mary V. Wakeman, *East Haddam*. Unpublished MS. n.d., East Haddam Free Public Library, East Haddam, Conn.

106. **relieved of the obligation of paying personal taxes**: Connecticut Colony 1850, 4: 261.

106. **founding member of the First Church**: See Parker 1938. A local historian associated with the church believes that the founding member may have been Daniel's son, also named Daniel (Karl Stofko, e-mail to author, June 19. 2009). Parker refers to both Daniels and is, for his part, definite about the founding role of "Daniel Cone, Sr."

106. **infamous witchcraft trials**: Noyes' "very instrumental" role is noted in Field 1814, 25.

106. **evidence of a spiritual conversion**: See Cunningham and Warner 1984, 4. For a complete account of this aspect of religious practice, also see Patricia Caldwell's *The Puritan Conversion Narrative* (1983).

106. **Little about her , including her maiden name**: Not Spencer, as is sometimes asserted. Rebecca Spencer was considerably younger than Daniel, as she was born in 1660 (and died in 1706). Moreover, Rebecca Spencer married John Tanner in July 1690 in Haddam.

106. **she was considerably Daniel's junior**: Rebecca is said to have been born 1650 in England. She married Daniel in August 1692 (http:// freepages.genealogy.rootsweb.ancestry.com/~hwbradley/ aqwg1090.htm#17747)

106. **returned there** [Haddam] **to live about 1695**: Parker 1938.

106. **a ferry**: Stofko, ca. 1977, 2.

106. **a deed conveying his Haddam property**: the complete document (which adds primarily legal and customary language) is in the transcription of W. W. (William Whitney) Cone (Cone 1903, 13).

107. **a local historian wrote**: see Hosford B. Niles, *The Old Chimney Stones of East Haddam*, 1871. 1976 reprint.

108. **6,500 Cone descendants**: W. W. Cone noted that 900 letters sent to Cone family members were unanswered, and "the records of those lines will be found incomplete and unsatisfactory" (Cone 1903, 4).

Appendix

110. **Cone ranked 3,337**: 65,000 names are listed in the database file provided online http://www.census.gov/genealogy/www/freqnames2k.html

	rank	count	prop100k	cum_prop100k	pctwhite	pctblack
CONE	3337	9824	3.64	55217.23	88.6	7.4

110. **Calhoun, the most common Americanized version**: database file at http://www.census.gov/genealogy/www/freqnames2k.html

110. **The standard source on Scottish names**: Black, G. F. (1946). *The surnames of Scotland; their origin, meaning, and history*. New York, The New York Public Library.

110. **"Mac" means "son"**: Ibid, 447.

110. **the family was driven into exile**: Ibid, 167.

About the Author

Joseph Sutton Cone was born in New Haven and educated at Hopkins Grammar School and Yale College, which would make him seem very much the son of Connecticut, as most of his Cone ancestors had been before. However, in the mid-1970s he moved to Oregon, completed graduate work at University of Oregon, and for more than 25 years has been a faculty member at Oregon State University. The assistant director of an ocean and coastal science program, Oregon Sea Grant, and a science communicator by training, he has produced creative works in many media, including documentary video and popular science books. One of the latter, *A Common Fate: Endangered Salmon and the People of the Pacific Northwest* was in a sense a homage to the salmon that, in the seventeenth century, surely nourished the pioneering first Cones in North America.

The author examining materials in the historical and genealogical collection of Rathbun Memorial Library, East Haddam, Conn., 2005. (Photograph by Leslie Lundborg.)

This book was designed and produced entirely by the author. The text of the book is composed in Bodoni Seventy-two, a modern revivial of an eighteenth century typeface.

Made in the USA
Monee, IL
30 October 2021